The Films of Roberto Rossellini traces the career of one of the most influential Italian filmmakers through close analysis of the seven films that mark important turning points in his evolution: *The Man with a Cross* (1943), *Open City* (1945), *Paisan* (1946), *The Machine to Kill Bad People* (1948–52), *Voyage in Italy* (1953), *General Della Rovere* (1959), and *The Rise to Power of Louis XIV* (1966). Beginning with Rossellini's work within the fascist cinema, it discusses his fundamental contributions to neorealism, a new cinematic style that resulted in several classics during the immediate postwar period. Almost immediately, however, Rossellini's continually evolving style moved beyond mere social realism to reveal other aspects of the camera's gaze, as is apparent in the films he made with Ingrid Bergman during the 1950s; though unpopular, these works had a tremendous impact on the French New Wave critics and directors. Rossellini's late career marks a return to his neorealist period, now critically reexamined, in such works as the commercially successful *General Della Rovere*, and his eventual turn to the creation of didactic films for television. Emphasizing Rossellini's relationship to cinematic realism, *The Films of Roberto Rossellini* also explores in depth the aesthetic dimensions of his working method.

The Films of Roberto Rossellini

CAMBRIDGE FILM CLASSICS

General Editor: Raymond Carney, Boston University

Other books in the series:

Sam B. Girgus, *The Films of Woody Allen*
Robert Phillip Kolker and Peter Beicken,
    The Films of Wim Wenders
Scott MacDonald, *Avant-Garde Film*
David Sterritt, *The Films of Alfred Hitchcock*

The Films of
Roberto Rossellini

PETER BONDANELLA

Learning Resources
Centre

Published by the Press Syndicate of the University of Cambridge
The Pitt Building, Trumpington Street, Cambridge CB2 1RP
40 West 20th Street, New York, NY 10011-4211, USA
10 Stamford Road, Oakleigh, Melbourne 3166, Australia

© Cambridge University Press 1993

First published 1993
Reprinted 1993

Printed in the United States of America

Library of Congress Cataloging-in-Publication Data is available
A catalog record for this book is available from the British Library

ISBN 0-521-39236-5 hardback
ISBN 0-521-39866-5 paperback

For Harry, *il miglior fabbro*

Contents

Illustrations

xi

Preface

This introduction to what I consider the most interesting and significant films by Roberto Rossellini, a small percentage of his total artistic production, aims at analyzing the truly original elements of Rossellini's style and defining the many ways in which he helped to shape the history of postwar Italian cinema. Until only a few years ago, critical discussions of Rossellini virtually ignored his work during the fascist period, but I trust my overview of Rossellini's career and the chapter devoted to a film from this period will demonstrate how mistaken such a perspective was. Although Rossellini himself constantly refers to a search for truth and realism in his cinema (and is universally acknowledged as the father of Italian neorealism), his notion of exactly what kind of "truth" could be conveyed by the art of the cinema evolved drastically until the latter part of his career when he abandoned the commercial cinema completely for work in the upstart medium of television.

This book considers only seven films, but I believe they are the films that will continue to define Rossellini's genius in the future or will be deemed crucial in explaining the evolution of his cinematic style regardless of the ideological foundation of the critic examining Rossellini's works. Although this new series on great directors is not the proper place for academic polemics, I have also tried to suggest in the notes how a number of critics, particularly those associated first with *Cahiers du Cinéma* and more recently with *Screen* and their Marxist followers in the United States, have used their interpretations of Rossellini's works in their polemical arguments with their intellectual or academic opponents. My own point of view should be apparent in this book, but I have tried to present all such critical perspectives in a fair and impartial light.

However, the focus of my study is Rossellini's cinema, not Rossellini's critics. Because the format of this new series does not permit a completely exhaustive consideration of every aspect of each individual film, I have chosen my emphasis in each chapter carefully so that when I cannot analyze a problem in depth, I have at least suggested its existence and encouraged further thought on it. My hope is that the style of the book will satisfy the general educated reader and that the intellectual level of the discussion will not disappoint the academic specialist and the student.

My thanks go to the general editor of the series, Ray Carney, and my editor at Cambridge, Beatrice Rehl. Mary Corliss of the Museum of Modern Art's Film Stills Archives and Guido Cincotti at the Centro sperimentale di cinematografia provided invaluable assistance in obtaining photographs. A grant from the Indiana University Office of Research and Graduate Development helped to defray the costs of the photographs and funding from the Center for West European Studies at Indiana University allowed me to complete this book.

I have dedicated this book to Harry Geduld, a gesture long overdue for his constant encouragement of my interest in Italian cinema. More years ago than either one of us will care to recall, I gingerly suggested to him that as there were practically no courses devoted to Italian film in the entire country, it might be a good idea for me to organize such a course at Indiana University. No colleague could have been a better friend or a more inspiring model to follow during the almost two decades that have passed since that time. I hope this book will meet Harry's high standards for readability and analytical insight.

I
Rossellini and Realism
The Trajectory of a Career

When Roberto Rossellini was born on 8 May 1906 into a very well-to-do Roman family, his father's involvement in the design and construction of the Cinema Corso, still one of the most important theaters of Italy's capital, was an auspicious coincidence that, in retrospect, seems to foretell his eventual choice of profession.[1] But little about Rossellini's early years will help explain why his name would eventually be inextricably connected to the moment in Italian cinematic history known as neorealism, or why his entire career would be continuously defined by controversial discussions over the relationship between art and realism, cinema and society. At the fashionable Collegio Nazareno where Rossellini attended high school, he made a number of friends who would later prove useful to his career: Marcello Pagliero, later to play the role of the Communist partisan leader in *Roma città aperta;* Giorgio Amendola, who was the son of one of Italy's most famous antifascist leaders and became an important member of the Italian Communist Party and delivered Rossellini's funeral oration on 6 June 1977; and Franco Riganti, who became a film producer in the fascist period and provided Rossellini with an entrée into the film industry.

As a result of his excellent social and economic position, his charming personality, and his good looks, Rossellini seemed destined to become a playboy rather than a film director, and there was always something of the nonchalance of the nonspecialist in his approach to the cinema. Rossellini was always fascinated by airplanes and racing cars. Given the emphasis upon the virtues of danger and speed proclaimed by both the avant-garde futurists and the Fascists in Italy at this time, it would be surprising if such daring qualities did not appeal to a young man of his breeding and disposition. When supervising the African aerial sequences of *Un pilota ritorna* in 1941–42, Rossellini amazed the troupe with his enthusiastic work in the planes with his cameramen, logging some two hundred hours in the sky. Much of his youth was spent around automobile racing, and even after he had achieved international fame in the immediate postwar period as a director, he persuaded Aldo Tonti, the cameraman of several of his films in that period (*Il miracolo, Europa '51*) to accompany him on the legendary Mille miglia automobile race in 1953.

Rossellini's career would be marked by successive love affairs, marriages, and scandals that would eventually fill international tabloids. It is therefore not surprising that the initial cause for his contacts with the film industry had as much to do with his interest in pursuing beautiful women as it did with his desire to work there. Around 1932, he met a young actress named Assia Noris, who was making her debut in a comic film. Noris was the daughter of Russian parents who had been born in prerevolutionary Petrograd, and she would soon become one of the Italian cinema's most attractive stars, often linked in romantic roles with Vittorio De Sica, perhaps the most important comic actor of the 1930s in Italy. She eventually married Mario Camerini, the most original director of film comedies during the fascist period, in which both Noris and De Sica often starred. Rossellini married Noris impulsively, but the marriage (celebrated in a Russian Orthodox church) was annulled only forty-eight hours after it had taken place. By the time Rossellini eventually married Marcella De Marchis in 1936, he had apparently spent most of the money he had inherited from his father and was forced to provide for his wife and family by actually going to work in the only profession that interested him and in which he knew numerous people who might provide him with sorely needed letters of recommendation – the cinema.

Rossellini began working as a sound technician, progressed to film editor, and gradually advanced to working on scripts with other directors before he achieved the post of assistant director and then director. Shortly after Rossellini entered the cinema, we find him making no less than six short films, only one of which still survives: *Dafne* (*Daphne*, 1936), about which little is known; *Prélude à l'après-midi d'un faune* (*Prelude to the Afternoon of a Faun*, 1936), a nature film inspired by Debussy's music; *Fantasia sottomarina* (*A Fantasy of the Deep*, 1939), the only one of these brief works extant; *Il tacchino prepotente* (*The Overbearing Turkey*, 1939); *La vispa Teresa* (*Lively Teresa*, 1939); and *Il ruscello di Ripasottile* (*The Brook of Ripasottile*, 1941). It was during Rossellini's work on these brief films that he received the crucial break of his early career, an invitation to collaborate on the making of Goffredo Alessandrini's *Luciano Serra, pilota* (*Luciano Serra, Pilot,* 1938) as assistant director and scriptwriter. Rossellini's introduction into Alessandrini's troupe probably had more to do with the fact that he was a friend of the producer, Franco Riganti, and of Vittorio Mussolini, who was supervising the film, than any wealth of cinematic experience on his résumé. Rossellini's collaboration with Alessandrini and his close friendship with the Duce's son raise one of the most interesting issues that critics must face in dealing with Rossellini's cinema – Rossellini's relationship to the fascist cinema and to important Fascists associated with the cinema.[2] This perplexing question leads to an even more intriguing critical problem – the relationship between the prewar cinema in fascist Italy and the postwar Italian cinema characterized by the rise of neorealism.

Fascist Cinematic Culture and Rossellini's Artistic Origins

The Italian cinema during the fascist period (1922–43) was virtually ignored by mainstream film critics and historians until only recently. Thus, in 1945, Cesare Zavattini, soon to become famous as the scriptwriter for Vittorio De Sica's greatest neorealist classics, declared that the two decades under fascist rule had not produced "a single film, let me say not one – that is, not 3,000 meters of film out of thirty million shot" – that was worth discussion. Carlo Lizzani, a neorealist director active as a film critic during the fascist period, asserted in his history of Italian cinema, which was, until a decade ago, the standard Italian text, that "not one photogram" of the hundreds of films made between 1938 and 1943 should be remembered or regretted if lost, since they constituted merely "a cold listing of commonplaces in a squalid and monotonous recipe book."[3] Italians were understandably anxious to forget the fascist years, which ended with the collapse of the regime and a bloody resistance struggle between 1943 and 1945 that assumed the proportions of a civil war before hostilities ended. Critics, film historians, politicians, and even veterans of the film industry who had learned their trades during the fascist period had every interest in emphasizing the originality and revolutionary quality of what succeeded the fascist cinema – Italian neorealism – and to denigrate everything that came before it. For three decades after the war until a retrospective in 1975 and a conference in 1976 inspired a fresh, new look at fascist cinema in Italy, the highly charged ideological climate in Italian intellectual life simply would not allow a dispassionate analysis of the period's film production. As a result, until recently the over seven hundred films produced during the fascist period were virtually ignored by scholars and critics, and this critical neglect

3

inspired by ideological blinders resulted in the eventual loss of the only remaining prints of almost half these films.[4]

Numerous traditional interpretations of the Italian cinema of the fascist period were immediately challenged by this new approach to the subject. The first and most immediate critical impression was that of surprise. Because practically no one had ever actually bothered to study the films in question, no one had ever imagined that so many were so good or that the average quality of the industrial product of the period was so high. In the second place, virtually all the ideological commonplaces about the period were immediately abandoned. The most significant outcome of this reevaluation of an entire period's cinematic production was the assessment of the role of political ideology in it. Virtually all recent studies of the films in question reject classifying it as a cinema of propaganda. In fact, these studies conclude that out of the over seven hundred films made, only a few can be called "fascist," although a larger number have patriotic or nationalistic themes.

Such a drastic reassessment of fascist cinema strikes directly at one of the most deceptive myths of Italian film historiography – the persistent interpretation of postwar Italian neorealism as a completely revolutionary and

Mussolini arrives to inaugurate the opening of Cinecittà, the heart of the commercial film industry during the fascist period, when Rossellini began his career in the cinema. *Source*: Cinecittà Archives

4

original phenomenon, the result of a clean and absolute break with both Italian film traditions under fascism as well as those classic "rules" established by the Hollywood model. As we shall see from our examination of Rossellini's major neorealist works, neorealism's relationship to its past and to the dominant cinematic language of Hollywood was far more complex than this myth of originality suggests. As a matter of fact, Italian film culture under fascism was a rich, multifaceted, and highly heuristic springboard for postwar cinematic production. The most obvious contribution of the fascist period to postwar cinema was to provide a well-trained and thoroughly professional cadre of directors, writers, and technicians no nation other than the United States could surpass. Mussolini's regime itself contributed a great deal to preparing the Italian cinema for its future with the foundation in 1935 of the Centro sperimentale di cinematografia, the professional film school that is still in existence, as well as the construction of the even more important studio complex of Cinecittà, which was inaugurated by Mussolini himself on 21 April 1937. Cinecittà remains today the focal point of Italian cinema and is one of only a few key studio complexes in Europe capable of rivaling Hollywood facilities. The day Mussolini selected for the inauguration of Cinecittà was significant, for the regime considered 21 April a national holiday, the anniversary of the founding of ancient Rome. Although the famous photograph of Mussolini behind a movie camera at Cinecittà with the motto "The cinema is the most powerful weapon" (a citation by Mussolini of Lenin) seems to reflect the regime's preoccupation with the cinema's propaganda potential, it was a potential exploited primarily in the famous newsreels produced by the fascist regime's Istituto Luce (an abbreviation for L'unione cinematografica educativa).[5] Only rarely were commercial films expected to reflect the regime's ideology. Most Fascists were content to allow the film industry to provide mass public entertainment.

Abundant evidence demonstrates that the fascist regime took a genuine interest in the health of the film industry and wanted it to flourish, without, however, insisting upon ideological purity in its products. In fact, the totalitarian regime's model was Hollywood, not the rigidly controlled popular culture of Soviet Russia or Nazi Germany.[6] In 1934, Luigi Freddi (1895– 1977), a former supporter of Marinetti's futurist movement and a staunch member of the Fascist Party since its foundation in 1919, was appointed director of the Direzione generale per la cinematografia, a bureau that was placed within the Ministero per la cultura popolare (commonly referred to as the "Minculpop"). Freddi later became president of Cinecittà in 1940. By all accounts, Freddi was an able administrator interested more in promoting a profitable, commercial industry much like that of Hollywood than

The figure of Mussolini at the inauguration of Cinecittà, presented as a director
peering through a camera lens to emphasize the importance his regime gave
the cinema, rises over Lenin's famous definition of the cinema Mussolini was
fond of quoting: "The cinema is the most powerful weapon." *Source*: Cinecittà
Archives

in directing a propaganda machine. In 1935, a special government fund for
the production of Italian films was approved by the Banca nazionale del
lavoro, and around the same time, Count Galeazzo Ciano, Mussolini's son-
in-law – undersecretary and then minister for press and propaganda – encouraged the creation of university film societies ("Cinegufs," clubs associated with the Gioventù universitaria fascista, or the GUF). In 1934, the
regime added cinema to the internationally famous arts festival in Venice
(the Biennale), and it consistently supported the development of an Italian
cinema to compete with its Hollywood model by sending its most important
ministers to the festival.

Perhaps the most consequential (even though indirect) link of Mussolini's
regime to the cinema was through the dictator's son Vittorio, who was
personally involved in production and scriptwriting. He was also the head
of a very influential film review, *Cinema,* around which a group of intellectuals gathered who were vigorous opponents of a cinema of amusement
and entertainment (paradoxically, the fascist regime's preference), and who
argued forcefully for a new cinema of realism that would be truly Italian.

6

The *Cinema* group included Giuseppe De Santis, Carlo Lizzani, Luchino Visconti, Michelangelo Antonioni, and Mario Alicata, to mention only those individuals who played a key role in the neorealist cinema of postwar Italy. Rossellini became a close friend of Vittorio Mussolini, and much of his success during the fascist period may be attributed to this personal connection.

The myth that the fascist cinema was primarily a cinema of ideological propaganda is based on the assumption that the regime preferred a cinema designed to mobilize the masses politically. In fact, the fascist regime preferred a successful commercial cinema based on the Hollywood model, complete with the star system, a collection of important auteur directors, and a genre-oriented subject matter.[7] Paradoxically, the voices calling for a realistic cinema employing documentary techniques with the goal of presenting "authentic," "believable," and specifically *Italian* landscapes or stories came from within the ranks of the left-wing Fascists as well as from the group around Vittorio Mussolini, most of whom became Communists after the fall of the regime. Although Vittorio Mussolini held strong views on Italian cinema, he rarely imposed them on the young intellectuals he protected. A perfect example of this fascist call for an anti-Hollywood brand of cinema with everyday realism as its goal can be found as early as 1933 in an essay called "The Glass Eye" by Leo Longanesi, an important journalist and writer who strongly supported the regime at the time:

> We should make films that are extremely simple and spare in staging without using artificial sets – films that are shot as much as possible from reality. In fact, realism is precisely what is lacking in our films. It is necessary to go right out into the street, to take the movie camera into the streets, the courtyards, the barracks, and the train stations. To make a natural and logical Italian film, it would be enough to go out in the street, to stop anywhere at all, and to observe what happens during a half hour with attentive eyes and with no preconceptions about style.[8]

Anyone comparing Longanesi's essay "The Glass Eye" with Cesare Zavattini's often-cited neorealist manifesto "A Thesis on Neo-Realism" will immediately be struck by the similarity of the two aesthetic positions.[9] The truth of the matter is that the fascist cinema began the search for cinematic realism; this impulse was later brought to fruition in the immediate postwar period when cinematic realism could benefit from the greatly increased freedom of expression after the fall of the regime.

Roberto Rossellini's apprenticeship in the cinema took place precisely when such an interest in a new cinematic realism was being expressed by a number of ideologically diverse individuals in Italy. A number of the techniques in his postwar neorealist classics have precedents in films made during the fascist period. The use of nonprofessional actors, so striking a technique in Rossellini's *Roma città aperta* (*Open City*, 1945) and *Paisà* (*Paisan*, 1946), and in the classic neorealist films of Visconti and De Sica, was masterfully employed by Alessandro Blasetti in his 1934 epic film *1860*, which sets the lives of ordinary people against the backdrop of Garibaldi's invasion of Sicily. Blasetti not only employed nonprofessionals but he allowed them to speak their Sicilian dialect, a use of authentic language that was practically unnoticed by film historians until Visconti did the same thing in his celebrated neorealist treatment of Sicilian fishermen, *La terra trema* (*The Earth Trembles*, 1948). The move from constructed studio sets to authentic outside or indoor locations, another of the traditional formulae associated with Italian neorealism, was frequently a feature of some of the most important of the films shot during the fascist period. Blasetti's *1860* is an excellent example of this on-location work, but even before this, in his silent *Sole* (*Sun*, 1929), Blasetti had celebrated Mussolini's reclamation of the Pontine marshes in an epic film regrettably destroyed during the last war. Augusto Genina's *Lo squadrone bianco* (*The White Squadron*, 1936) was shot on location in Libya and contains very beautiful desert sequences. The most impressive sequences of Walter Ruttman's *Acciaio* (*Steel*, 1933) were shot inside the giant steel mills at Terni and are masterful examples of rhythmic editing within a semidocumentary style typical of many neorealist films. Mario Camerini's early comedy *Gli uomini, che mascalzoni!* (*What Rascals Men Are!* 1932) contains remarkable location footage of the city of Milan and its industrial fair that traditional criticism has not usually associated with the comic genre or with Camerini. *Luciano Serra, pilota* contains remarkable African footage that Rossellini supervised as Alessandrini's assistant director. The simple fact is that the use of nonprofessional actors, real locations, and documentary techniques was part of a growing trend toward film realism in the fascist cinema even before the advent of neorealism, and it is doubtless in this context that Rossellini learned of the effectiveness of such techniques.

When Italy entered the Second World War in June 1940, the film industry there (as in Nazi Germany, Great Britain, and the United States) was expected to do its bit to assist the war effort, providing not only newsreels but also popular entertainment that bolstered the regime's political and ideological goals. As a result, the most innovative aesthetic experiments in the cinema at the time involved what have become known as "fictional documentaries."[10] Essentially, such films would employ documentary footage and authentic locations (battleships, airfields, military outposts) from the war, combining them with a fictional framework; in some cases, nonprofessional actors were employed (the actual protagonists of the events portrayed), and in other instances, famous actors appeared with ordinary sailors, soldiers, and airmen.

Perhaps the most influential impetus to this kind of filmmaking, a model Rossellini could not have ignored, was the phenomenal success of a film of this type begun even before war broke out and released in 1940: Augusto Genina's *L'assedio dell'Alcazar (The Siege of the Alcazar)*, a film that led all others at the box office during that year.[11] It was awarded the Mussolini Cup at the Venice Biennale for the Best Italian Film of the year, and although its political content might cause us to question the validity of such an award, the film won abundant praise for its innovative cinematic qualities from none other than Michelangelo Antonioni, writing in the leftist journal *Cinema*. He underlined the film's lack of rhetoric, its grounding in recent history, and his opinion that the film's value sprang from its creation of an "epic feeling" from believable acts of sacrifice and drama by single individuals. Of particular interest is Antonioni's comment that the film has a "choral" quality (one of the most typical descriptions of Rossellini's work in the fascist period and the immediate postwar neorealist era).[12] Antonioni also notes that Genina successfully uses the group of soldiers and civilians defending the Alcazar fortress for Franco's army against an overwhelming force of Republican soldiers to create a microcosm (he calls it a "small city") of life that permits the intensification of emotions and drama within a tightly controlled and almost claustrophobic cinematic space. Rossellini would do something very similar in his own "fascist trilogy" and even more brilliantly in the torture sequences of *Roma città aperta*.

The cinematic merits of *L'assedio dell'Alcazar* are real, just as its clearly ideological tone cannot be ignored. In a prologue, the viewer is told that the heroic defense of the Alcazar was a symbol of the ideological struggle of Franco's fascist forces against bolshevism in Spain. The prologue insists, however, that the story is reported with historical accuracy, a claim that may be generally accepted. Nevertheless, Republican soldiers are depersonalized and depicted as ugly, brutal, and treacherous, taking hostages and executing prisoners without much remorse, whereas the defenders of the fortress are portrayed as honorable military officers obeying the rules of "civilized" warfare. There is nothing in *L'assedio dell'Alcazar* that should shock the viewer of the usual run-of-the-mill American combat films during the same period. Few national cinemas were able or willing to portray the enemy in a positive light. The interior scenes were constructed at the Cinecittà studios, and the exterior scenes were completed on location at the Alcazar amidst the ruins that still remained when the footage was shot. The texture of the photography and the skillful reproduction of the interior sets, combined with on-location Spanish footage, give practically no hint that the film was not entirely done on location.

The "fictional documentary" quality of the film arises from the distinctive rhythm that Genina produces by alternating between dramatically re-created battle scenes and more intimate moments inside the fortress that reveal the unfolding of sentimental dramas. Actual documentary footage of such historical events as the bombing of the fortress by the Republican air force is also skillfully edited together with the footage Genina produced. The dramatic appeal of the film derives from a highly traditional story of the conflict between love and duty, honor and sacrifice. A rich, spoiled woman named Carmen (Mireille Balin) who has taken refuge in the Alcazar becomes transformed and learns to work for the common good by nursing the wounded, thereby attracting the attentions of the film's stalwart military hero, Captain Vela (Fosco Giachetti), who can love her only when she realizes that she must embrace the Fascist virtues of discipline and self-sacrifice.

The critical problem in a film such as *L'assedio dell'Alcazar* was perceived by everyone, especially the Fascist officials who would have to bear the responsibility of a commercial failure if the large sums of money invested in Genina's film did not make a profit. Luigi Freddi read the script before production began, and in a letter to Renato Bassoli, the producer, Freddi defines the script as a "fictional documentary" ("*un documentario romanzato*") and worries about the combination of the realistic or historical part of the film with its fictional or emotional part:

> While it is certain that the part which we have defined as "documentary" (that is, the real events recreated by technical and artistic means) attains a very high emotional content (from which, however, arises a serious defect, as I will explain later), the imaginative part, that is the dramatic part in the sense of the spectacle, the part created expressly to connect the evocation of historical events with the unrelated human events, seems to me to be very weak.[13]

The completed film was certainly more successful in combining history and fiction than Freddi had predicted from a reading of its script. In fact, Alessandro Pavolini, Fascist minister of education and later Freddi's successor at the Direzione generale per la cinematografia, wrote Genina a congratulatory letter, calling the film a "service to the country" and remarking that technically, the work was "in no way inferior" to the best films made in the world, Hollywood included, in its reconstruction of battle and crowd scenes, and it was "decidedly superior" in its "respect for historical accuracy, elegant sobriety and human emotion."[14] Nevertheless, the critical problem Freddi identified even more clearly than Antonioni did in his very positive review – the aesthetics of combining "real" events from history with "fictional" events – will remain central to an understanding of Rossellini's filmmaking from his debut with the so-called fascist trilogy in 1940–43 to the production of his neorealist trilogy in 1945–47, which established his international reputation as a serious and innovative auteur.[15]

L'assedio dell'Alcazar was a purely commercial venture. But the other fictional documentaries produced before the fall of the regime in 1943 were frequently associated directly with various branches of the Italian armed forces. The Istituto Luce produced newsreels, and the army, navy, and air force all had cinema departments, although the army produced very few films. In the naval ministry, at the Centro cinematografico del Ministero della marina, a man of genius, Francesco De Robertis (1902–59), took the lead in championing the marriage of fiction and documentary. Vittorio Mussolini (also a captain in the air force in addition to his work in the cinema) was a stimulating presence in the air force's Centro fotocinematografico del Ministero dell'aeronautica. Rossellini worked with both departments, making a film for each of them before he made the third film of his fascist trilogy without military support. The navy sponsored three films: two by De Robertis, Uomini sul fondo (Men on the Bottom, 1940) and Alfa Tau! (1942); and Rossellini's first feature film, La nave bianca (The White Ship, 1941). All three were produced with Scalera Film, a commercial company. The air force produced three more works: Rossellini's second feature, Un pilota ritorna (A Pilot Returns, 1942); Mario Mattoli's I tre aquilotti (The Three Young Eagles, 1942), for which Rossellini's brother, Renzo, wrote the musical score and on which Roberto may have worked without credit; and Esodo Pratelli's Gente dell'aria (People of the Sky, 1943). The first two films were scripted by Tito Silvio Mursino, an anagram for Vittorio Mussolini; the last was supposedly written by Bruno Mussolini, Vittorio's brother killed in an air accident in 1941. The cinematic style Rossellini evolved out of his relationship to De Robertis and his work with the armed forces, as well as the political ideology contained in his fascist trilogy, will be analyzed in Chapter 2, devoted to L'uomo dalla croce.

Unlike De Robertis, who went north after the fall of the fascist regime in 1943 to work for the industry associated with the Republic of Salò (thereby destroying any hopes he might have entertained of returning to the commercial cinema after the war), Rossellini was far too clever and far less devoted to the fascist cause to compromise his future with such a dramatic act of political commitment. After the war, the decision to follow the fascist government north became the litmus test for individuals compromised by their relationship to the fascist regime and its cinema. Those who went north, like De Robertis, rarely were able to return to the industry after the war, whereas the fascist connections of individuals who stayed in Rome, such as Rossellini, were basically ignored. Between the fall of the fascist regime in September 1943 and the Allied liberation of Rome in June 1944, Rossellini became closely attached to the group of leftist critics associated with *Cinema* and worked on a film tentatively entitled *Scalo merci (Freight Station)* written with the assistance of Giuseppe De Santis, who had collaborated with Luchino Visconti on *Ossessione (Obsession, 1942)*, a film postwar critics would view as one of the important precursors of neorealism. *Scalo merci* originally intended to portray the working-class atmosphere of the San Lorenzo district of Rome, where the train station for freight was located, but after the Allied bombardments destroyed the station, Rossellini was forced to modify the setting. He decided to move the film to an area populated by woodsmen in order to transport the entire production closer to Allied lines and therefore to safety. It is difficult to call the film Rossellini's since much of the film was changed by Rossellini's friend Marcello Pagliero, who became famous for his role as the partisan leader in *Roma città aperta*. The film was released in 1946 with the title *Desiderio (Desire)*.

After the liberation of Rome from the Germans in June of 1944, Rossellini collaborated with a number of scriptwriters, including Sergio Amidei and Federico Fellini, on a project about life under German occupation. After a number of major changes in the script, shooting began in January of 1945, under the worst possible conditions. When *Roma città aperta* appeared that September, it was met with universal critical and popular approval and ranked first in the box-office listings for the 1945–46 season, one of only several neorealist classics to reach a wide, popular audience. When the film was exported to the United States in February of 1946 and was shown at the first Cannes Film Festival that year, its astonishing commercial and critical successes continued, making Rossellini an immediate international celebrity and giving birth to the phenomenon of Italian neorealism. With the imposition of this work by an unknown Italian director upon the international market, Italian neorealism was forever after identified with Rossellini, and not a few of the misunderstandings about his future career would be the result of this hasty identification.

Fast on the foreign success of this film, Rossellini began the production of what would be a far more original and seminal contribution to the neorealist epoch, *Paisà*, written with the collaboration of Amidei, Fellini, Klaus Mann (the son of the famous German novelist), Vasco Pratolini (a Florentine writer identified with literary realism), and several others. The work consisted of six different sequences tracing the Allied invasion of Italy, and Rossellini filmed at a number of locations (although not always authentic ones, as many theories of neorealism are fond of emphasizing) throughout Italy. At least one account of Rossellini's rationale for the choice of locations has attributed it to the director's pursuit of a new mistress!

In fact, now that Rossellini was an international celebrity, his private life was fast becoming all too public. His affair with Roswita Schmidt (who played a major role in *L'uomo dalla croce*) ended, but not before Rossellini had persuaded both his mistress and his wife to sell their jewels to assist him in raising money for *Roma città aperta*. On 14 August 1946, Rossellini's son, Romano, suddenly died. At almost the same time, his friend Anna Magnani delivered a son with infantile paralysis. Rossellini probably met Magnani years earlier on the set of *Luciano Serra, pilota*, since Magnani was then the wife of the film's director, Alessandrini. The grief the two felt apparently drew them together into a stormy affair that lasted until 1949,[16] when Rossellini began his equally infamous love affair with Ingrid Bergman. Magnani's starring role in *Roma città aperta* threw the two together in the numerous personal appearances they made following the film's debut, and by the time the couple journeyed together to Paris in 1946 after triumphs at Venice and Cannes, Rossellini's visit to the French capital turned into a critical apotheosis of his work as well as a public confirmation of his new love affair with Magnani.

In both Italy and France, an ideological and critical controversy was brewing over the proper direction Italian cinema should take and the definition of Italian neorealism. Conservatives attacked neorealist films for their brutal realism that projected abroad what they perceived as a willfully negative image of Italy, while leftists praised Rossellini, De Sica, and Visconti for such a dismal portrait and urged the cinema to continue in its democratic, antifascist, and progressive direction. Ideologues on both the Right and the Left tended to privilege a single definition of Italian neorealism that fast became a critical formula rather than a tentative, neutral critical analysis,

Rossellini and Anna Magnani during the years of their love affair. *Source*: Museum of Modern Art Film Stills Archives

a prescription rather than a description: nonprofessional actors, authentic locations, documentary photography, contemporary subject matter, the rejection of Hollywood genres, and a leftist perspective defining film as a force for social change rather than as a kind of amusement became a litmus test applied to every new director or film. *Roma città aperta* and *Paisà*, Rossellini's seminal films of the neorealist trilogy, will be examined in detail in Chapters 3 and 4.

Quite naturally, Rossellini was among the first directors to object to any kind of a critical straitjacket, and his films after *Paisà* almost immediately set off in what was perceived as a radically new direction. His work would involve a more intimate cinema with emphasis on the psychological workings of the lonely individuals it portrayed, and it would have a decidedly Christian temper that would enrage the same leftist critics who so strongly supported the social messages of his neorealist trilogy. In Paris, Rossellini met Jean Cocteau and decided to film the French playwright's play *La voix humaine*. His American distributor, Joseph Burstyn, who had successfully distributed the first two works in the neorealist trilogy, encouraged Rossellini to do a version of the Italian-American novel *Christ in Concrete* by Pietro Di Donato (eventually done by Edward Dmytryk in 1952). At the same time, Rossellini considered filming a version of Richard Wright's *Native Son*. A Roman historical film on the evil empress Messalina, scripted by Federico Fellini, was also announced but never begun during this period.

Rossellini's search for a different kind of cinematic language that would depart from the programmatic realism demanded by some Italian and French critics can be seen in *Germania anno zero* (*Germany, Year Zero*, 1947), even if this third part of the neorealist trilogy is set amidst the ruins of bombed-out Berlin. The German project was interrupted in order to complete another project, *L'amore* (*Love*, 1948), even though *Germania anno zero* was actually released a year before *L'amore*. *L'amore* consists of two brief films exploiting the acting talents of Anna Magnani. One is an adaptation of Cocteau's play with Magnani delivering the long, dramatic monologue of a jilted mistress on the telephone with the lover who is abandoning her for another woman. Oddly enough, this is exactly the situation in which Rossellini would soon place Magnani herself after Ingrid Bergman's famous telegram reached Rossellini as he was completing work on *L'amore*. The Cocteau adaptation was joined to another brief work, entitled *Il miracolo*, written by Federico Fellini, in which Magnani plays a demented peasant girl who meets a mysterious stranger (played by Fellini with a blond beard) she takes to be Saint Joseph. When he leaves her, she discovers she is pregnant, declares her child to be a miracle, and, after being rejected by the townspeople, withdraws to a deserted sanctuary to deliver her baby.

The Cocteau adaptation was probably more revolutionary in terms of cinematic style, for in it Rossellini began his experiments with a cinema of psychological introspection that is characterized by extremely long takes, organizing actions normally filmed in a series of shots tied together by montage editing with a single complex take, concentrating the entire force of the episode upon a single actress, her facial expressions, and her individual suffering. In fact, this is the direction he would later take with the five films he made with Ingrid Bergman. But it was *Il miracolo* that created a clamorous scandal, as conservatives and religious bigots attacked Rossellini for what they considered a blasphemous parody of the Immaculate Conception. In America, Rossellini attracted the ire of no less a figure than Cardinal

Spellman, as well as the American Legion. Some of the anger directed toward the film was no doubt inspired by the notoriety of the love affair between the director and Bergman, which became public knowledge by the time Burstyn released *L'amore* as *The Ways of Love* with two other brief works by Jean Renoir and Marcel Pagnol. Although the film passed the censorship of the New York Regents, a government official lacking any legal authority in New York City overruled the board and ordered the theater to stop screening the film or lose its license. Burstyn decided to take the case to court, and on 26 May 1952, the United States Supreme Court ruled for the first time that films were not merely a business but were a means of expression protected by the First Amendment. Moreover, because the state was not charged with protecting specific religions from criticism (in this case, Roman Catholicism), sacrilege could not be an excuse for artistic censorship.[17]

Rossellini insisted in an interview a few years later that *Il miracolo* was "an absolutely Catholic work" and remarked that it embodied a theme that obsessed him not only in this work but in others he made during the period – "the absolute lack of faith ... typical of the postwar period."[18] Rossellini admired the faith of the dim-witted peasant girl played by Magnani because she embodied the essential ambiguity of true religious sentiment and set into relief its inevitable conflict with conventional wisdom in the everyday, workaday world. He shared this essentially Christian view of the world with his scriptwriter Fellini, who was to have much greater success with this theme in two Oscar-winning works only a few years later, *La strada* (*La Strada*, 1954) and *Le notti di Cabiria* (*The Nights of Cabiria*, 1957). *Il miracolo* shows Rossellini exploring new directions for the new Italian cinema that he would follow in the five films he made with Ingrid Bergman in the 1950s. But another film begun after *Il miracolo*, *La macchina ammazzacattivi* (*The Machine to Kill Bad People*) also suggests new ideas and experiments in style in its metacinematic exploration of the power of the camera (the *macchina* of the title). This too often ignored comic film was begun in 1948, but work was interrupted on several occasions. *La macchina ammazzacattivi* was finally released in 1952 and will be analyzed in Chapter 5.

Rossellini's interest in the role of Christian values in the contemporary world also inspired the making of *Francesco, giullare di Dio* (*The Flowers of St. Francis*, 1950), an adaptation of the collection of popular legends surrounding Saint Francis (the medieval book entitled *I fioretti di San Francesco*). After the uproar over *L'amore*, Rossellini employed Fellini again in this production as a scriptwriter but put two Catholic priests to work as well. These two individuals, Félix A. Morlion, S.J., and Antonio Lisandrini, O.F.M., lent an air of theological respectability to the production even if they actually contributed very little to the script. Morlion was a strong defender of the *Catholic* foundations of Italian neorealism, which he naturally found better expressed in the cinema of Rossellini and eventually of Fellini than in films produced by leftist directors. In his essay "The Philosophical Basis of Neo-Realism," first published in 1948 by *Bianco e Nero*, the official journal of Rome's Centro sperimentale di cinematografia, Morlion remarks that "in Italy, intelligence, imagination, and sensitivity are immensely creative because they are linked to a simple and rich human tradition, the fruit of twenty centuries of heroism and sacrifice: the Christian tradition. There is only one danger for the neo-realist school: a loss of contact with the deep source of human reality, which in Italy is either Christianity or non-existent."[19] Rossellini was never a practicing Catholic, but he always admired the ethical teachings of the church and was fascinated by religious sentiment, which was too often ignored in the materialistic world he inhabited.

The Bergman Period: Toward a Spiritual Dimension of Reality

While Rossellini was working on *La macchina ammazzacattivi*, in Los Angeles Ingrid Bergman quite by chance went to see a film everyone was discussing in America *(Roma città aperta)*. She was so struck by it that a few months later in Paris she went to a deserted art house to see Rossellini's *Paisà*. Afterward, she wrote Rossellini a letter, which reached him on 8 May 1948, his fortieth birthday:

> Dear Mr. Rossellini,
> I saw your films *Open City* and *Paisan,* and enjoyed them very much.
> If you need a Swedish actress who speaks English very well, who has not forgotten her German, who is not very understandable in French, and who, in Italian knows only "ti amo" I am ready to come and make a film with you.[20]

Although it is doubtful that Rossellini was actually thinking of Bergman for a film at that moment, he gallantly replied that he had been doing so for some time, and in a subsequent letter to her, he proposed a meeting in Paris to work on the details of the proposed film. In this second letter, he warned Bergman not to expect the kind of Hollywood script and tight production schedule she was accustomed to from her work in America: "I want you to realize that my method of working is extremely personal. I avoid any kind of script that, in my opinion, limits enormously the field of action."[21] It seems that Bergman really did not understand exactly how different Rossellini's working habits were from the industrialized, highly ordered studio system in Hollywood, for Rossellini was forced to send her another letter in November to explain himself more clearly. In it, he enclosed only a brief outline of the proposed film, what later became *Stromboli, terra di Dio* (*Stromboli, Land of God*, 1949), justifying the almost nonexistent script by the fact that he usually worked from a few basic ideas, developing them little by little as he worked on the set, and stating that individual scenes were often inspired by reality while he worked.[22]

Even though Rossellini knew that his methods would not satisfy Hollywood producers, he nevertheless accepted financing for his new picture from Howard Hughes and RKO, and this Hollywood connection would later prove to constitute a major problem. In fact, in retrospect, it seems clear that Rossellini intended to accomplish two important operations with Bergman. On the one hand, after the neorealist era emphasized nonprofessional acting performances, he wanted to restore the actor to a central position of importance, something he had already attempted with Magnani in *L'amore*. An expressive acting performance far beyond the possibilities of most nonprofessionals was absolutely crucial to his new themes of spiritual poverty and problems of human communication. This centrality of the actor, of course, flew in the face of the often-expressed preferences for nonprofessional actors voiced by many critics and movie directors associated with Italian neorealism, and Rossellini's selection of Ingrid Bergman would therefore provoke negative reactions in some circles. On the other hand, by employing Ingrid Bergman, the archetypal female star of *Casablanca*, in a film artistically light-years removed from a Hollywood commercial style, Rossellini intended to provoke a significant change in direction within Italian cinema, until then dominated in the critical literature by calls to promote an Italian brand of neorealist social (and sometimes socialist) realism and at the box office by Hollywood imports.

Rossellini completed five films starring Ingrid Bergman between 1949 and 1955: *Stromboli, Europa '51, Viaggio in Italia, Giovanna d'Arco al rogo,* and *La paura.* In addition, during this period, he made a film designed as a vehicle for the great Italian comic actor Totò, entitled *Dov'è la libertà...?* (*Where Is Liberty...?* 1952–54). He also completed a number of briefer films, including *L'invidia* (*Envy*), the fifth episode of a work entitled *I sette peccati capitali* (*The Seven Deadly Sins,* 1952); *Ingrid Bergman,* a brief sketch in a film devoted to film actresses entitled *Siamo donne* (*We, the Women,* 1953); and *Napoli 1943* (*Naples 1943*), an episode of *Amori di*

18

Rossellini, Ingrid Berg-
man, and their family.
Source: Museum of
Modern Art Film Stills
Archives

mezzo secolo (*Mid-Century Loves*, 1953). The scandal of his love affair
with Ingrid Bergman was intensified with the birth of their son, Robertino,
born out of wedlock on 2 February 1950, and their subsequent marriage
by proxy in Mexico on 24 May 1950, a marriage that the Catholic church
never recognized. In 1952, the twins Isabella and Isotta were added to the
family.

It is not surprising, given the importance of this relationship in Rossellini's
personal life, that problems of communication between married people and
the issue of solitude, grace, and spirituality in a world without moral values
become the central themes of Rossellini's Bergman films. But perhaps even
more important was the extremely clever use Rossellini made of his wife in
films, defying audience expectations. In *Stromboli*, for example, Bergman
portrays Karin, a northern European refugee who marries a Sicilian fish-
erman to escape a refugee camp. When she arrives on the volcanic island
in the Mediterranean that is to be her home, she discovers a totally alien
culture and moral values far removed from those of the north. As she tries

to escape up the rocky, barren landscape of the volcanic mountain in the closing sequences of the film, she comes to realize the meaning of the child within her body that will soon be born, turns to God, invoking his mercy, and returns home to her husband. Shot on an authentic island location in accord with formulaic definitions of neorealism, the film was made under extremely primitive conditions, with no indoor plumbing or hairdresser for the star. There was practically no script either, as Rossellini preferred to improvise dialogue while shooting progressed; there were also no available doubles, so that Hollywood's most famous actress was obliged to do difficult and even dangerous scenes herself. In short, as one critic has noted, Rossellini employed Bergman *as if* she were a nonprofessional.[23] While the religious overtones of the film's conclusion quite naturally provoked negative critical reaction on the Left, the revolutionary techniques Rossellini employed in shooting this film and the other works with Bergman went largely unnoticed. These techniques would become a seminal influence upon avant-garde cinema of the 1960s and included a use of landscape that anticipates the great films of the mature Antonioni, juxtaposing barren locations with the emotions and psychological developments of his protagonists. Moreover, by this time in his career, Rossellini had already adopted the extremely long take as his characteristic signature with the camera, and he had decisively rejected traditional dramatic structures that work upon the audience's emotions in favor of a more alienating, distancing effect. One immediate result of this drastic modification of his film style was that Rossellini's works immediately lost their appeal with the broad, commercial audiences that had flocked to the theaters all over the world to see *Roma città aperta*.

Europa '51 (1951) continues Rossellini's exploration of the possibilities of his wife's talents. Bergman has remarked that this film (scripted in important sections by Federico Fellini, who is never credited for his contributions) continued the religious theme of Rossellini's earlier *Francesco*. Bergman's character, Irene, is employed to demonstrate that in today's world, the simple religious faith of the early Franciscans is totally incomprehensible to a wide range of ideologies and traditional institutions and can only be understood as a form of mental illness. The sudden death of Irene's son shocks her into examining her comfortable, middle-class life; she begins to help the poor and the needy, even filling in for a day at a dreary factory job for an unmarried woman with too many children; eventually her efforts to practice Christian charity cause her to be declared insane by the courts, a verdict with which her relatives, the representatives of the church, and even her Communist cousin agree. If the religious conclusion

Rossellini and his crew filming the most famous of all his sequences in an authentic location: the last sequence of *Paisà* in the Po River Valley. *Source*: Centro sperimentale di cinematografia Photograph Archives

of *Stromboli* was offensive to some anticlerical critics, the reaction to this film was even more negative. Viewed today, however, it is an indictment of an intellectual and moral atmosphere characterizing a specific time and place – Europe in the immediate postwar period in the midst of a crisis of ethical values.

Rossellini's subsequent work *Viaggio in Italia* (*Voyage in Italy*, 1953) was greeted with unanimous negative attacks in Italy and was a commercial flop, whereas the young critics associated with *Cahiers du Cinéma* in France praised it so extravagantly that they ranked it as one of the greatest films of all time. Although no film can ever live up to that kind of exaggerated praise, *Viaggio in Italia* is nevertheless universally recognized today as the most innovative film of the Bergman period. As it will be examined in detail in Chapter 6, it suffices here to note that this work embodies Rossellini's distaste for and avoidance of traditional cinematic spectacle in favor of what some critics have called "a neorealism of the person" in its focus upon psychological states of mind, marital conflict, and the link of characters to their environment (again, a theme to be exploited with greater popular success by Michelangelo Antonioni in the next decade).

Meanwhile, Rossellini was experimenting with the direction of musical theater. On 13 December 1952, his production of Verdi's *Otello* opened in Naples at the Teatro San Carlo. Subsequently, he would produce other operatic or dramatic works, including Amilicare Ponchielli's *La gioconda* (1953); Gabriele D'Annunzio's *La figlia di Jorio* (1954); a musical version of Arthur Miller's *A View from the Bridge* scored by his brother, Renzo (1961); and a production of Beniamino Jappolo's *I carabinieri*, with sets and costumes designed by the famous realist painter Renato Guttuso, that would later inspire Jean-Luc Godard's film, *Les carabiniers* (1963). One of the Bergman films of the period was a color version of an oratorio Rossellini staged first in Naples and then in the major capital cities of Europe: *Giovanna d'Arco al rogo* (*Joan of Arc at the Stake*, 1954). This was a version of Paul Claudel's and Arthur Honegger's oratorio *Jeanne au bûcher* that originally appeared in 1939. Once again, Rossellini deliberately capitalizes upon Bergman's celebrated performance as Joan of Arc in a Hollywood interpretation of the historical figure by employing Bergman in the same role but portraying her in a completely non-Hollywood, anticommercial style. When this film failed at the box office and with the critics, and when *La paura* (*Fear*, 1954), an adaptation of a novella by Stefan Zweig, met an equally disastrous fate, it seemed as if Rossellini's career was finished in the cinema. Moreover, Rossellini's nonconventional casting of his wife in his various cinematic experiments was being blamed for ruining the career of one of the world's great actresses. Bergman, too, was anxious to return to the commercial cinema. There is good reason to believe that she had never really understood Rossellini's rejection of traditional Hollywood canons of acting, dramatic structure, and audience response, and when she was offered the lead role in *Anastasia* and accepted it against Rossellini's wishes, who wanted her at home or working only in *his* films, the stage was set for the dramatic break of what was, until the romance between Elizabeth Taylor and Richard Burton, the postwar period's most-publicized love affair.

Rossellini became understandably discouraged with the commercial cinema after this series of box-office failures, although it must also be admitted that it was naive of him to believe he could present nontraditional and even anticommercial films to traditional audiences with great success, even if these works starred one of Hollywood's greatest leading ladies. Between February and October of 1957, Rossellini went to India to film a documentary for Italian and French television at a time when most famous directors absolutely avoided association with this upstart medium of mass communication. In an important interview conducted by André Bazin with Jean Renoir and Rossellini, Rossellini declared that television offered the director "enormous freedom," since movie audiences had become contaminated by a "mass psychology," whereas television viewers were "individuals" and the director's relationship with his audience was more "intimate."[24] Although in light of much contemporary research on mass-market television such a statement seems naive, nevertheless the opportunity to do for a strange and exotic culture in *India* what Rossellini had earlier done for Italy in *Paisà* was an attractive challenge at a moment when only the enthusiastic young critics in France, such as Jacques Rivette, François Truffaut, André Bazin, Amédée Ayfre, Eric Rohmer, and Jean-Luc Godard, championed his films.[25] Living in Paris between June 1954 and December 1956, Rossellini was treated most deferentially by this group of *cinéastes*, who considered him a *maître à penser* and a model to follow in their own cinematic experiments precisely because of his disdain for traditional cinematic conventions.

History and Television: Rossellini and the Rejection of Commercial Cinema

Rossellini's *India* received favorable reaction from the Cannes Film Festival in 1957 and gave the director new credibility with producers. Rossellini's Indian experience also introduced a new mistress (Sonali Senroy, the wife of his Indian producer) to replace Ingrid Bergman, who had returned to her former career in Hollywood. Once again, his private life became the target of tabloids and scandal sheets. By the time he obtained a legal separation from Bergman in November 1957, his new companion was already pregnant, giving birth to their daughter Raffaella at the end of the year. Even though *India* marks the direction Rossellini's career would eventually take toward television documentaries, financial considerations led Rossellini to turn first to four commercial films that may be termed a "historical tetralogy": *Il generale Della Rovere, Era notte a Roma, Viva l'Italia,* and *Vanina Vanini*. In addition, he made a brief documentary on the city of Turin and an important but little-known episode entitled *Illibatezza*, part of a film with the strange title *Rogopag*, an anagram of the last names of the four directors, who each contributed a different episode (Rossellini, Godard, Pasolini, Gregoretti).

Of the four "historical" films, only *Il generale Della Rovere* (*General*

Rossellini on the set of *Il generale Della Rovere*, preparing the execution
sequence against the obviously artificial canvas backdrop that announces his
departure from earlier on-location shooting typical of his neorealist classics.
Source: Centro sperimentale di cinematografia Photograph Archives

Della Rovere, 1959) can be considered a critical as well as a commercial
success. Its intriguing return to the demands of commercial cinema with
Vittorio De Sica in a brilliant starring role not only earned a Golden Lion
Award at the Venice Film Festival in 1959 but also made a great deal of
money. In this fashion, Rossellini responded to those of his critics who
declared he could not narrate a conventional story (even though, as the
analysis of the film in Chapter 7 will demonstrate, the story is only deceptively conventional). *Era notte a Roma* (*It Was Night in Rome*, 1960) has
often been denigrated as a simple remake of *Roma città aperta*, for it returns
to the year 1943 and the German occupation of the Eternal City to narrate
the tale of three Allied prisoners hiding in a Roman apartment. This film
is most remarkable for its heavy use of the Pancinor zoom lens technique,
which Rossellini had first introduced in *Il generale Della Rovere* and which

would characterize the rest of his career, just as the long take and the tracking shot were the hallmarks of his Bergman period. With the Pancinor technique (actually invented by Rossellini), the length of a take is limited only by the amount of film stock the camera holds; it decreased editing costs by eliminating the extensive use of montage; and aesthetically, it added a number of additional expressive possibilities to the art of the cinema. Paradoxically, as one critical discussion of its use underlines, the zoom always calls attention to itself as a cinematic device of artifice and illusion while, at the same time, increasing the possibilities of "realism" in the cinema.[26]

For the centenary of Giuseppe Garibaldi's liberation of Sicily, the Italian government commissioned Rossellini to do a film on Italy's Risorgimento hero, and the result – *Viva l'Italia!* (*Garibaldi,* 1960) – was relatively successful at the box office. But *Vanina Vanini* (1961), the subsequent film, taken from Stendhal's *Chroniques italiennes* (1829) and also treating the Italian Risorgimento, was another box-office disaster. Rossellini made *Anima nera* (*Black Soul,* 1962) in a desperate attempt to recoup his losses, and when it failed miserably, even he declared that the film was terrible. But by this time, his grandiose historical project of filmmaking for television had become a reality, and Rossellini was able to abandon for the rest of his career the demands of the commercial cinema that had never really appealed to his sense of individual freedom or his contempt for commercial considerations. Something of his discontent can be seen in *Illibatezza* (*Chastity,* 1962), which is a metacinematic discourse on the role of the movie camera and an indirect attack upon the rather naive doctrine of cinematic realism put forth by some of the neorealist theorists decades earlier. With this final ironic look at a commercial art form he would forever abandon, Rossellini sets out on an entirely new and perilous course, one no other filmmaker had ever explored.

Cinema as a Didactic Tool: Rossellini's Later Career

Beginning with *L'età del ferro* (*The Iron Age*) in 1964 and continuing in this same vein until his death in 1977, Rossellini produced eleven major works of an essentially didactic nature that were conditioned by the medium of television.[27] Many of these films involve massive amounts of time on screen, ranging from four to twelve hours, and are made up of a number of separate episodes. They reflect what Rossellini's biographer has defined as the *cinema-saggio,* or the film essay, abandoning the traditional idea of a dramatic protagonist for a pedagogical look at a great man in history, usually representative of an age in which some profound psychological shift in human consciousness occurred (Socrates, Blaise Pascal, Louis XIV, Cosimo de' Medici, Augustine, Descartes, Alcide De Gasperi, and Jesus Christ). When Rossellini died, he was planning several equally ambitious projects, films on Karl Marx and the American Revolution. This period in his career also coincides with a massive outpouring of letters, interviews, and articles on his views about the cinema and, most particularly, in defense of a didactic cinema for television.

Rossellini was one of the first major film directors to move to the medium of television and to defend his decision to do so on intellectual grounds. A number of his aesthetic positions in this regard are worth mentioning. In the first place, while attempting to reconstruct historical realities of past eras with as little distortion by ideology as possible, Rossellini nevertheless completely rejected cinema verité, at the time a favorite technique of some of his French admirers, especially Jean Rouch. For Rossellini, even documentary films implied artistic interpretation, the fundamental rational element of filmmaking for Rossellini, whereas cinema verité embodied in essence a refusal to interpret. Moreover, in a rather heated Parisian debate in 1963, Rossellini argued that the French fascination with the camera and with cinematic technique was a sign of artistic weakness and lack of ideas. Only a moral position, and not a mechanical technology, could grasp the truth.[28] Explicitly rejecting the desire to be considered an avant-garde artist or an experimenter, Rossellini preferred to be considered a craftsman making a product (the didactic film) that could instruct and enlighten millions of individuals. His design was not unlike that great educational project of the European Enlightenment, the *Encyclopédie,* which was intended to broaden the base of human knowledge and to extend it to the masses who were ignored by the elitist system of education. Not the least of the advantages of this turn to television, however, was Rossellini's freedom from commercial restraints. Because the RAI, the Italian public television network, enjoyed a protective state monopoly during the time Rossellini produced films for this medium, he was practically guaranteed a huge audience that had little choice but to watch his films or turn off the set. Moreover, Rossellini's legendary quickness in shooting a film now became one of his greatest virtues as a director for television. In almost no time at all, Rossellini could complete a series of episodes in a television program, assisted by his technique of long takes and his frequent use of the zoom to limit the amount of editing necessary. His acknowledged masterpiece for television, *La prise de pouvoir par Louis XIV (The Rise to Power of Louis XIV,* 1966; see Chapter 8), was completed in only twenty-four days in August 1966 and was presented almost immediately to the Venice Film Festival in September of the same year, winning Rossellini both critical and popular praise and confirming him in the choice of his artistic direction for the rest of his career.

Rossellini's first television film, *L'età del ferro*, traces the history of iron and steel from the Iron Age to the present day in a five-part series. Although Rossellini's son Renzo is listed as the director, there seems little doubt that Rossellini was completely responsible for the grand design and the artistic approach to the subject matter. The most interesting aspect of this particular film is not its history of the steel industry but its fictional reconstruction of the atmosphere of *Roma città aperta* and *Paisà* in a tale of a steelworker's dealings with the Germans and the Italian Resistance. Half of the cost of the film's production was covered by a subsidy from the Italian state company Italsider, and Rossellini's next and most successful television film, on Louis XIV, would be financed by the ORTF, French public television.

Rossellini's focus on the French monarch produced a far more satisfying work of art than did his more grandiose didactic themes following the pattern of his history of iron and steel. In *La lotta dell'uomo per la sua sopravvivenza* (*Man's Struggle for Survival*, 1967–69), a massive twelve-part series that was made over a long period (1964–70), during which time Rossellini interrupted work to make both the film on Louis XIV and one on the Christian apostles, Rossellini covered the history of humanity from prehistory and the agricultural revolution through the Bronze Age; the rise of Egyptian, Greek, and Roman civilizations; the barbarian invasions; the appearance of Islam; the Middle Ages and the Renaissance; the origins of modern science and technology; and the era of great inventions (radio, the telegraph, electricity), down to the advent of space travel. When it was finally shown on Italian and French television, it received a low audience share and has attracted little critical attention since that time. *Atti degli apostoli* (*The Acts of the Apostles*, 1968) fared somewhat better with the television public. In this film, made on location in Tunisia and employing a cast of nonprofessionals for all but the roles of the apostles, Rossellini eliminates almost all the miracles reported in the New Testament, thus showing us apostles who are historical figures rather than saints. Rossellini apparently saw Christianity more as a stage of human development than as a revealed truth, and in his next television film, he would turn to the contribution of Greece in *Socrate* (*Socrates*, 1970). Before working on this ambitious project, he completed a brief documentary on Sicily for the NBC network in the United States.

In 1968 at the height of the political upheavals convulsing Italian society, Rossellini was named to head the Centro sperimentale di cinematografia, the state-operated cinema school in Rome, which had been adversely affected by the tumultuous political events in the capital. As a nonconformist film director, he was considered the perfect candidate in an era of cultural crisis, but most descriptions of his tenure there reveal how he actually helped to weaken the professionalism of the school's curriculum by abolishing courses on direction, releasing many old instructors, and emphasizing personal experimentation rather than institutionalized instruction. Perhaps Rossellini considered the school the embodiment of everything in the commercial film industry he detested, but his so-called reforms did not effectively assist the students he sincerely admired to pursue their careers in a commercial industry. There was more than a bit of the populist demagogue in Rossellini's stay at the Centro and even a tinge of patronization, for although his own career reflected the value of experimentation, it was also based on long experience in the commercial industry that none of his students had yet enjoyed. His relationship with the Centro continued until 1973. Certainly more important for his career was the relationship that arose between Rossellini, a Houston-based foundation, Rice University, and the NASA establishment in Texas. As the overall design of his television films demonstrates, Rossellini had become fascinated with the history of scientific and technological progress, and where better than the rocket capital of America could Rossellini capture the spirit of this new and exciting human odyssey projected toward other worlds? Rossellini would actually pass several of his last years in Houston, planning new projects and learning more about contemporary technology.[29] He was called there by Texas philanthropists Jean and Dominique DeMenil, who were interested in establishing a Media Center at Rice University designed to inject a critical element into audiovisual communication rather than merely supply the commercial film industry with trained specialists. The attempt to increase public access to the Media Center evolved into an organization called the Southwest Alternate Media Project, which is still in operation today. *Rice University*, a documentary film of almost two hours in length, contains a number of interviews Rossellini had with scientists at the university that demonstrate the director's interest in employing audiovisual media to explain science to large commercial audiences of nonspecialists.

Rossellini's ambitious program of didactic television films proceeded even as he was developing his contacts in America. His *Socrate* was received favorably at the 1970 Venice Film Festival, where two other major made-for-television films by Fellini (*I clowns* [*The Clowns*], 1970) and Bertolucci (*La strategia del ragno* [*The Spider's Stratagem*], 1968) were also presented. The fact that Rossellini had been a pioneer in moving from cinema to television was not overlooked by other Italian directors, who soon realized that the RAI had become one of the few purely Italian sources of film funding available to them. *Socrate* was followed in rapid succession by other projects: *Blaise Pascal* (1972); *Agostino d'Ippona* (*Augustine of Hippa*, 1972); a documentary of a conversation with Salvador Allende, the Socialist president of Chile, shown on Italian television on the evening in 1973 of Allende's overthrow; *L'età di Cosimo de' Medici* (*The Age of the Medici*, 1972), a portrait of the marriage of politics, economics, art, and philosophy in Quattrocento Florence; and *Cartesius* (*Descartes*, 1973).

Rossellini's last two feature-length films tackle two extremely controversial subjects. In *Anno uno* (*Italy: Year one*, 1974), Rossellini provides a sympathetic portrait of the most important Italian politician of the postwar era, Alcide De Gasperi, the statesman from the Christian Democratic Party who resolutely guided Italy toward democracy within the framework of NATO and a free-market, anticommunist government. The outraged cries of critics from the Left proved that it was far easier for Rossellini to treat historical periods distant in time than it was to apply Rossellini's television techniques to the contemporary era, when the protagonists were still, for the most part, alive. It appears that Rossellini intended to provoke both the right and the left wings of Italian political culture, for he planned a filmed biography of Karl Marx (never begun), and in 1975 he completed a biography of Jesus Christ, entitled *Il Messia* (*The Messiah*, 1975).

One of Rossellini's last contacts with the official cinema of festivals and prizes was his presidency of the jury at the Cannes Film Festival in 1977. He was primarily responsible for the award of the Grand Prize to *Padre padrone* by the Taviani brothers. It is likely that Rossellini supported the work not only because of its intrinsic merits but also because it was produced for television, and it must have represented a bittersweet victory to him and a vindication of the struggles of his later career to witness a television film carrying off the most important prize at a festival devoted to the art of the cinema. Shortly thereafter, on 3 June 1977, Rossellini suffered a massive heart attack and died at the age of seventy-one, still bubbling over with various projects that he was not permitted to complete – films devoted to Mao, the conquistadores in Latin America, Marco Polo, the encyclopedists, the American Revolution, and many other subjects.

Rossellini's funeral three days after his death seemed a return to the days of political compromise celebrated by his most popular film, *Roma città aperta*. His body was first laid out in a communist Casa di cultura, and then a church funeral followed, where the heads of the Christian Democratic and the Communist parties – Aldo Moro and Enrico Berlinguer – sat together, architects of the so-called historical compromise that was to be shattered in the next year by Moro's assassination. Giulio Carlo Argan, the mayor of Rome and distinguished Marxist art historian, managed to mispronounce no less than three times the name of the deceased, changing his name from Roberto to Riccardo!

Roberto Rossellini was a remarkable individual. He helped bring about a revolution within Italian cinema with neorealism, a film style he practically created. Italian neorealism would dominate the artistic development of Italian cinema for years to come and still has a profound influence upon young directors in Italy. Then, he led the way toward a very different kind of introspective neorealism of the person with the films he made with Ingrid Bergman. These films were rejected by the public and by most Italian critics, but they were embraced by the younger generation of French film critics associated with the *Cahiers du Cinéma*. By his influence upon these budding film directors who would make up the French New Wave, Rossellini's work once again had a profound effect on the development of world cinema. At the same time, in such often-neglected works as *La macchina ammazzacattivi* or *Illibatezza,* Rossellini began to question the power of the movie camera. And finally, as if to astound his critics still further, Rossellini turned back to commercial cinema and produced one of the best historical films of the postwar period, *Il generale Della Rovere,* before abandoning the commercial cinema forever and embracing the didactic potential of films for television. Here, too, his masterpiece on the rise to power of the French monarch Louis XIV established new aesthetic boundaries for television films to which other directors could only hope to aspire.

The French critics that idolized his personality and canonized his works may have been mistaken in their intellectual assessments of Rossellini's originality. But they were completely correct in grasping the fundamental principle of Rossellini's entire life, something that his greatest pupil, Federico Fellini, had already discovered years before on the set of *Paisà:*

> I think I may honestly say that what I mostly owe to Roberto Rossellini's teaching is his example of humility, or better, a way of facing reality in a totally simplified way; an effort of not interfering with one's own ideas, culture, feelings.... when I came in touch with Rossellini, I saw at first a completely new world, the loving eyes through which Rossellini observed everything to make things alive through his framings. It was actually through his attitude that I thought that, after all, films may be created without deceits, without presumptions, without thinking of sending around quite definite messages.... I definitely realized that the camera, the film apparatus on the whole are not so

very mysterious, so terribly technical. It was just a matter of relating quite simply what one was looking at.[30]

Fellini and the young film buffs in Paris soon to become the French New Wave were not alone in seeing Rossellini as a model. A number of Italian directors of the generation after Rossellini (Gillo Pontecorvo, Ermanno Olmi, the Taviani brothers, Bernardo Bertolucci, and Pier Paolo Pasolini) became convinced through the force of Rossellini's example that the cinema could become a means of personal, artistic expression rather than merely a commercial medium of industrialized entertainment. Ultimately, Rossellini's greatest lesson is not a principle of cinematography or a special technique. Instead, his artistic legacy is a moral and didactic object lesson that the art of the cinema is ultimately a branch of the humanities and that great cinema has much to teach us about the meaning of the human condition.

2
L'uomo dalla croce
Rossellini and Fascist Cinema

Of the three films in Rossellini's so-called fascist trilogy celebrating the armed forces of the fascist regime, *La nave bianca* and *Un pilota ritorna* reflect the direct involvement of the Italian navy and air force. Only *L'uomo dalla croce* was shot without the direct collaboration of a branch of the Italian armed services, nor did Rossellini's friend Vittorio Mussolini contribute anything to its script, as he had done on *Un pilota ritorna*.[1] However, Rossellini used the services of Asvero Gravelli, who, unlike Mussolini's son Vittorio, was an authentic Fascist ideologue who had been a leading exponent of an international fascist movement after the model of the Communist Internationale and who was closely associated with two major fascist journals, *Antieuropa* and *Gioventù Fascista*.

Rossellini himself had always explained his political background and first encounter with fascism by an anecdote recounting his father's remarks in 1922 when Mussolini first came to power. As Rossellini told the story, his father peered out the balcony at the celebrating black-shirted Fascists below who had just completed the famous March on Rome, and he remarked in disgust: "Children, remember that black hides dirt very well."[2] Like so many other members of the wealthy upper middle class and the aristocracy, his father's antifascism was more a matter of aesthetics than of passionate political commitment. It is clear that Rossellini was relatively unconcerned with the moral issues associated with the Fascists' hold on power in Italy until the war began to go very badly for Italy and, later, when his own life was actually in danger during the German occupation of Rome from September 1943 until the city was liberated in June 1944. It must not be forgotten that it was in large measure due to Rossellini's personal relationship with Mussolini's son Vittorio that Rossellini was able to insert himself into the Italian film industry with so little difficulty or such lack of previous experience.

The critical issue involved here is not to determine whether *L'uomo dalla croce* is a fascist film. Almost all reputable critics are in agreement that very few, if any, Italian films made between 1922 and 1943 actually reflect pure fascist ideology. That is to say, there are few films that embody the regime's truly original political ideas. There are, of course, a number of excellent films that embrace Italian nationalism, praise the bravery of the nation's soldiers, and support Italian culture as a civilizing influence abroad in its empire. But the key concepts of Italian fascism and the ideas that mark the movement as an original method of mobilizing and organizing a nation during a period of rapid industrial and economic development – the corporate state; the rejection of both liberal parliamentarianism and Marxist class struggle; the definition of Italy as a "proletarian" nation with a right to a place in the sun and an empire; the notion that a nation can prove its character only in military conflict; and the philosophical position that life itself is struggle – are conspicuously absent from the films of the period.[3]

The recognition that most films made under fascism, and even those "fictional documentaries" such as Rossellini's wartime fascist trilogy, are not completely fascist in character still calls for clarification of Rossellini's intentions in making a work such as *L'uomo dalla croce*. Although it is no longer possible after the critical reevaluation of fascist cinema over the past two decades to identify Italian cinema during this period as an ideological cinema, it is also true that all too many of Rossellini's postwar critics have glossed over Rossellini's personal and intellectual links to the regime, and not a few read into *L'uomo dalla croce* certain attitudes that picture Rossellini in an all too favorable light – that of a potential antifascist artist and intellectual. However, such an interpretation not only obscures Rossellini's own naive, confused, and often self-interested political values but also underestimates the traumatic effects of the German occupation of Rome and the partisan Resistance upon Rossellini. It is perhaps enough to say that immediately after the fall of the fascist state on 25 July 1943, there were a number of Italians who suddenly discovered themselves anti-Fascists, or at least hastened to avoid mention of their previously close ties to the regime and its leaders, whereas before that date they had been completely at home in the drawing rooms and salons of the regime's officials. Rossellini must certainly be numbered as one of these individuals, even though it is equally difficult to doubt the sincerity of his sudden "conversion" to making neorealist films in the immediate postwar period that are identified with an entirely different political ideology.

Certainly no official in the fascist regime would have imagined that in a few short years, Rossellini would become identified with an antifascist cinema. In 1941, Rossellini's first feature film, *La nave bianca*, was awarded a special jury prize at the Venice Biennale: the Cup of the National Fascist Party. Both its commercial success and its skillful adoption of the fictional documentary techniques of Francesco De Robertis had almost overnight made Rossellini a favorite with the public, the press, the producers, and the government. *Un pilota ritorna* continued this success, in part due to the presence in the film of one of the period's most important dramatic stars, Massimo Girotti. Thus, when Rossellini began shooting *L'uomo dalla croce* in July 1942, there was every reason to believe that his career would continue its meteoric course with a third film on the Italian armed forces. In fact, in his postwar memoirs, Luigi Freddi actually singles out Rossellini for praise as the director the regime considered in the most favorable light possible:

> This director – from his collaboration on the script of *Luciano Serra, pilota* to the direction of *La nave bianca* and *Un pilota ritorna* and a project for a film on Francesco Crispi – was perhaps the only man who decisively turned toward the film of political propaganda and war. He was actually directing one of these films, *L'uomo dalla croce,* whose plot was intended to glorify a military chaplain and which unfolded in Russia during the campaign by the Italian expeditionary force, and whose realization took place with nonprofessional actors (and perhaps an improvised script), when the production company found itself in troubled waters. L'ENIC was then forced to take over the production and the Cines Company to take it under its wings. The making of the film thus marched on a more secure track and the film was completed with the result that we all know.[4]

The timing of such a film speaks volumes about Rossellini's political naiveté. *L'uomo dalla croce* was shot between July and September of 1942 and was released in June of 1943, only a month before the Allies invaded Sicily. It was not surprising that the film was withdrawn almost immediately. But one wonders what could possibly have been going through Rossellini's mind in mid–1942 when he set out to make such a film. Hitler's armies in Russia and the very Italian expeditionary force his film portrayed were driven disastrously and decisively onto the defensive by the Russians at Stalingrad in the last weeks of that year. Releasing a film celebrating the "victories" in Russia must have taken a great deal of sangfroid for even a nonpolitical person such as Rossellini. It seems incredible that Rossellini did not see the handwriting on the wall with the fall of Libya in January 1943, after which the invasion of Sicily was expected by everyone even before Rossellini's film was actually released in June. The invasion, taking place on 10 July 1943, was the specific catalyst that moved the Fascist Grand Council to depose Benito Mussolini as dictator of Italy after a reign of over two decades.

The man with a cross, the protagonist to which the film's title refers, was a figure based upon a real army chaplain, Father Reginaldo Giuliani, who had actually been killed in action on the Russian front. Rossellini's plot will remind anyone who has seen *Roma città aperta* of that later and more illustrious film focusing upon the antifascist exploits of a partisan priest, likewise based upon an actual person who fell in the struggle against the Nazis during the German occupation of Rome. The earlier film's structure is deceptively simple. As the film opens, we are introduced to the various members of an Italian tank unit stationed on the Russian front during the summer of 1942 (that is, before the disastrous defeats of the Axis powers there). The mood of these troops is one of self-confidence in eventual victory, and their material and spiritual conditions are superb. We naturally see none of the infamous defective equipment or the summer uniforms issued for winter combat that so many Italian veterans of this campaign have emphasized. There is certainly no hint of impending military disaster. More-over, the normally overbearing Nazi allies are completely absent from view during the entire film. And even more surprising to a non-Italian audience that has, no doubt, been regaled by traditional stories about Italian military incompetence in every military campaign, including that in Russia, the ef-ficiency, professionalism, and skill of the Italian officer corps and the rank-and-file soldier are above reproach. In fact, at the conclusion of the film, we witness a decisive Italian victory over the Russians. But all of this is clearly not Rossellini's main focus. Instead, he concentrates on the selfless heroism of a military chaplain who volunteers to stay behind with a seriously wounded Italian tankman when his unit must abandon the man and move forward to the attack. The chaplain's action means certain capture by the Russians. In fact, on the following day, the chaplain and the wounded soldier are taken by Russian troops to be interrogated by a Communist officer, who has another young Italian found with a Fascist Party card in his pocket executed on the spot for refusing to answer his questions. Too late to save the young man, the Italians attack the Russians, and the village where the priest has been interrogated is trapped between the two hostile armies in battle. The priest drags his wounded tankman inside a small farm building, a Russian *izba,* where he encounters a group of Russian peasant women with their children, who are eventually joined, first, by a group of Russian partisans led by a commissar named Sergei and his girlfriend, Irina, and, later, by some Italian tankmen who abandon their burning vehicle, surprise the partisans from the rear, and take control of the *izba*. They, in turn, are joined by Fyodor, a terribly disfigured Russian soldier, burned in a tank explosion, who, by a strange coincidence, was Irina's former lover before she met Sergei. Fyodor kills Sergei in a fit of jealousy just as Sergei is attempting to overpower the Italians inside the hut. The chaplain helps to deliver a baby, baptizes it with the Christian name of Nicola, teaches the children to make the sign of the cross, explains his religious faith to an incredulous Irina (who is grieving over the death of Sergei), and is finally mortally wounded attempting to save Fyodor's life just as the victorious Italian troops retake the Russian village.

Each of the three films in Rossellini's fascist trilogy stands in a slightly different relationship to the general formula of the fictional documentary genre that was initiated by De Robertis. In *La nave bianca*, Rossellini skill-fully combines documentary footage of an actual naval battle he shot himself with footage of daily life on Italian warships, and as a result, much of the film possesses the feel of authentic newsreel documentary film. To this documentary or pseudodocumentary section of the film, Rossellini then added a more conventional fictional story (that of a sailor and his sweetheart, who becomes a nurse, and whose paths cross on a hospital ship where the sailor has been brought after being wounded in combat). Thus, he combined real locations, documentary style, and nonprofessional actors with a con-ventionally sentimental or melodramatic plot. In *Un pilota ritorna*, the nonprofessionals are replaced by one of Italy's most celebrated matinee idols, Massimo Girotti, but the other actors were newcomers to the screen, and much of the shooting was done at an airfield in Viterbo (not the Greek front, but as close to an authentic location as possible). Once again, however, the film's plot moved in the direction of fiction rather than documentary. *L'uomo dalla croce* continues Rossellini's progress within the trilogy toward a preference for fiction over documentary. In it, there is no documentary footage at all – the battle scenes are re-created by the director near Ladispoli outside Rome, where he constructed an entire Russian village and staged a firefight worthy of the best Hollywood war scenes. But the battle scenes, unlike those in *La nave bianca,* are precisely that – *scenes* of combat that we consider "realistic" insofar as they follow traditional Hollywood pre-scriptions for war films. Although the battle sequences are brilliantly con-trived examples of Hollywood "realism" rather than authentic footage of an actual battle (such as occurs in *La nave bianca*), to some extent Rossellini

Convincing re-creations of combat scenes on the steppes of Russia filmed in the Roman countryside by Rossellini for *L'uomo dalla croce*. *Source*: Centro sperimentale di cinematografia Photograph Archives

returns to the use of the nonprofessional actor in this film. The military chaplain is played by a friend, Alberto Tavazzi, who was an architect and set designer. The part of Irina was given to Rossellini's girlfriend, Roswita Schmidt, a dancer (not an actress). And many of the film's characters are certainly not professional actors.

Most critical discussions of Rossellini's fascist trilogy make use of a critical term, *coralità*, or a choral quality,[5] which the director himself used to describe these films in an often-cited (but imperfectly understood) interview given in 1952 to Mario Verdone:

> I have no formulae or preconceptions. But if I look back on my films, undoubtedly I find elements in them that are constant and that are repeated not programmatically but, I repeat, naturally. In particular, a choral quality. The realistic film is intrinsically choral. The sailors of *La nave bianca* count as much as the people hiding in the hut at the ending of *L'uomo dalla croce*, as much as the population of *Roma città aperta*, and as much as the partisans of *Paisà*.[6]

The most complex critical issue suggested by this statement is Rossellini's frequent contention that there is no essential difference between his "fascist" and "neorealist" films, an issue we shall discuss in a subsequent chapter. But here, it is important to understand exactly the kind of quality *coralità* implies. A chorus is a group that sings in unison, with no individual voices being discerned from within the collective whole. In other words, *coralità*, just as current Italian dictionaries suggest, represents the polar opposite of "individual." In short, it is precisely the kind of fascist military or ideological virtue that the regime celebrated. And Rossellini is entirely correct to claim that *coralità* is a quality in *La nave bianca*, for in that film, he recorded the activities of the sailors and the movements of the machines onboard ship during the naval battle with a montage-type form of editing that all critics have seen as influenced by Sergei Eisenstein. A single shot of one of Mussolini's famous political slogans painted inside the ship – *"uomini e macchine un sol palpito"* ("men and machines, a single heartbeat") – provides an exact definition of the choral quality Rossellini celebrated in this film. Rossellini's dramatic editing forces the viewer to see the sailors as essentially machines, small cogs in a gigantic war machine that work in unison and in harmony for the common goal of a naval victory. In essence, machine and man fuse into a single entity.

Nothing could be farther from the spirit of *L'uomo dalla croce* than this *coralità,* for in the third part of the fascist trilogy, Rossellini clearly gives prominence to an individual protagonist as opposed to a chorus of heroes, the "man with a cross" of the title. The only aspect of the film that might justifiably be called "choral" occurs in the first few sequences of the work as we are introduced to the tank unit and, for a few brief moments, are given insight into the daily lives of the rank-and-file soldiers there. As soon as the unit returns from the battlefield and the problem of the wounded soldier too sick to be moved is presented, the chaplain steps forward and the rest of the film emphasizes his individual selflessness, courage, and eventual martyrdom.

In spite of the understandable desire on the part of sympathetic critics to portray this chaplain as a symbol of the "feeling for freedom that conditions the whole film,"[7] Rossellini's chaplain embodies a commitment not to freedom but, rather, to the traditional and sometimes quite opposite virtues of duty, self-sacrifice, nationalistic patriotism, and Catholic morality that were also praised by the fascist regime, as well as by any government at war. It is, in fact, this nationalist, even jingoistic quality of *L'uomo dalla croce* that strikes most contemporary viewers of the film as its most unacceptable and alien feature, one too often hastily identified with fascist ideology. Nevertheless, Rossellini requires the viewer of *L'uomo dalla croce* to accept his assumption that following the moral code of Catholic Christianity, a doctrine elevating self-sacrifice and love for one's neighbor over even our own existence, entails an ethical choice of heroic proportions. The religious commitment portrayed links this work within a trilogy on the horrors of war to Rossellini's neorealist classics as well as to the various films made during the immediate postwar period with Ingrid Bergman.

Sometimes the tone of the film can become extremely heavy-handed. For example, after the chaplain is captured by the Russians, he is interrogated by a thoroughly despicable political commissar. The chaplain speaks Russian and can communicate with the Russians, but we are surprised to discover that the commissar speaks Italian as well, and although Rossellini leaves unanswered the mystery of how all this can be conceivable, the possibility is clearly suggested that the Communist commissar is an Italian traitor, one of the many Marxists who fled to Russia after the establishment of the fascist regime in Italy.[8] This figure represents the most blatant stereotype of a murderous Bolshevik one can imagine. Not only does he order the execution of a young soldier solely for his possession of a Fascist Party card, but he calls the chaplain a witch doctor and implies that all religion is merely superstition (a theme that Irina will later continue after the death of Sergei). To complete the portrait, the commissar suffers from a disgusting skin disease. His physical deformity reflects a deeper moral depravity that also characterizes Fyodor, Irina's ex-lover and the assassin of Sergei. Although the fact that Fyodor has been horribly disfigured in a burning tank may reflect a touch of realism, Rossellini employs this physical trait to underline his unwholesome character, and it is clear that the director prefers the brave and committed Communist partisan Sergei, who stands and defends his beliefs like a man, to Fyodor, who shoots Sergei in the back just as he attempts to take control of the hut in the middle of the village.

In fact, there is very little attempt to view both sides of this struggle with a dispassionate perspective. Rossellini considers communist ideology contrary to the moral tenets of Christianity and believes it deserves to be destroyed. The closing intertitle of the film, shot against the cross on the uniform of the dead chaplain, leaves no room for moral ambiguity: "This film is dedicated to the memory of the military chaplains who fell in the crusade against those without God in defense of their country and in order to bring the light of truth and justice even to the land of the barbaric enemy."[9] The iconography of the final scene before the intertitle, the chaplain with blood on his brow like the scourged Christ, clearly suggests Christian martyrdom. This image embodies the same traditional religious iconography that Rossellini will later employ in depicting the tortured Communist partisan leader Manfredi in *Roma città aperta*. It is important to note that Rossellini does not juxtapose communist ideology to fascist ideology in *L'uomo dalla croce*. Instead, he views Christianity as a neutral ethical standard that transcends all forms of political philosophy.

The practical demonstration of Christian morality and its superiority to a political interpretation of human existence is provided by the action taking place inside the Russian *izba*. Rossellini employs the hut as a kind of moral no-man's land between the two opposing armies and their conflicting ideologies. The combat scenes preceding the isolation in the hut are realistically convincing re-creations of battle, not dissimilar to those in dozens of American World War II films. But any pretense of following a documentary style is abandoned by Rossellini once he turns his attention to the individuals inside the hut, for here the entire narrative unfolds within a clearly melodramatic context. The chaplain's heroic stature is depicted in a conventional manner we usually identify with Hollywood narrative. He risks his life to find water in order to baptize the newborn Russian child; he divides his care between wounded Italians and Russians alike, regardless of their political affiliation; he even tells Irina that Sergei may well be with God after death, since he was a good man, and that she must have faith, for Christ died for everyone.

The mechanism that creates all of the emotional tension inside the hut is a familiar one, the melodramatic amorous triangle between Irina, Sergei, and Fyodor. We are not given all the information we need to understand the situation completely (just as we are not told everything about the Russian commissar who may be an Italian national), but Irina's sorrowful account of how Fyodor ruined her life twice (earlier in Moscow before she met Sergei and now that he has murdered him) suggests all sorts of narrative possibilities – that Fyodor was her first husband (the most innocuous), that Fyodor was her lover (the most likely), or even that Irina was exploited sexually by Fyodor, perhaps even driven into a life of prostitution (an outside possibility but one not to be discounted, given the theme's popularity in melodrama). At any rate, the suggestion seems clear: Irina's former life with Fyodor was one of degradation and despair, but Sergei changed all of that. Now after his death, Irina believes there is no hope left. The priest, of course, maintains that hope resides in Christian faith, not in human relationships, and that without faith, Irina is deader than Sergei.

As more than one critic has noted, an early review of *L'uomo dalla croce* by Giuseppe De Santis appearing in the journal *Cinema*, the major voice in the call for the creation of a new form of cinematic art in Italy, complained that Rossellini had not provided the proper "rhythm" in blending the two

The melodramatic conflict between Irina, the Russian partisan soldier, and her former lover inside the microcosm of the war symbolized by the Russian *izba*. *Source*: Centro sperimentale di cinematografia Photograph Archives

The Italian chaplain tries to reassure Irina with a Christian message after the death of Sergei, the partisan leader who was her lover. *Source*: Centro sperimentale di cinematografia Photograph Archives

aspects of the film, the documentary and the fictional/sentimental. De Santis was especially critical of the rhetorical, conventional, and traditional suspense that Rossellini created by focusing his attention on the human tragedy unfolding within such a concentrated and almost claustrophobic space inside the hut.[10] Representatives of the avant-garde, such as De Santis, and not a few of Rossellini's more recent critics, who want so badly to identify Rossellini's cinema with a modernist narrative style, frequently equate the presence of traditional, Hollywood-style narrative situations or characters in a film with an inferior or reactionary aesthetic design. They view the manipulation of an audience's emotions through melodramatic situations as beneath the contempt of the true avant-garde artist. In taking such a critical position, these critics fail to understand the almost hypnotic attraction of commercial cinema following the Hollywood model to even such an independent-minded director as Rossellini. We must remember that Vittorio Mussolini wanted to reform Italian cinema by making it more like Hollywood, not by abandoning the generic formulae that permitted Hollywood to capture the imaginations of heterogeneous populations all over the world. In fact, as we shall discover in the chapters devoted to Rossellini's neorealist classics, Rossellini does not completely abandon the most obvious vestiges of the commercial cinema even in *Roma città aperta,* and it is only in *Paisà* that a move away from conventional narrative structures becomes his overriding concern.

Many critics of *L'uomo dalla croce* have attempted to see hints of Rossellini's more revolutionary style in various aspects of the film. The very first shot of the film has been singled out more than once.[11] In it, Rossellini provides an extremely long, slow pan that follows birds in flight at springtime down to the ground where the Italian soldiers are bathing in a stream. He also uses long takes during the opening "documentary" sequences that capture the Italian soldiers operating their tanks or going into battle with flamethrowers. And again, in the evening just before the chaplain is captured by the Russians, there is another beautiful long take where the camera pans from the stars to an owl in the trees, then to a fox hiding in the bushes, and finally to the chaplain sitting with the wounded tankman, who has regained consciousness and asks to see the stars. But these long shots are conspicuous by their rarity in the work. To say that they foreshadow Rossellini's postwar style, which avoided montage in favor of the long take, is most certainly a critical exaggeration.

The most accurate assessment of the place of *L'uomo dalla croce* in the development of Rossellini's mature cinematic style would describe the film

The chaplain comforts a dying Fyodor, before losing his own life in a heroic Christian gesture. *Source*: Centro sperimentale di cinematografia Photograph Archives

as a predominantly traditional film containing tentative experiments in cinematic realism in its efforts to re-create authentic battlefield conditions, its use of nonprofessional actors, and its attempts to join documentary-style sequences typical of the newsreels with sequences constructed upon a fictionalized storyline. But traditional cinema clearly overshadows experimentalism, and Rossellini continues to exploit the generic conventions of the war film identified with Hollywood. His narrative is contained within an ideological package characterized by strong feelings of patriotism and a clear commitment to a notion of Christianity based on self-sacrifice and selflessness.

Realistically, it would be impossible to expect Rossellini to create a completely revolutionary cinematic style in only his third feature film, especially in a work made about wartime in a country ruled by a fascist government that intended, although it did not always succeed, to be totalitarian in nature. Rossellini's cinematic style would become revolutionary soon enough in the postwar period, but attempting to see a precursor of this distinctive stylistic signature in one of only several long takes in *L'uomo dalla croce* pays no interesting critical dividends. Instead, we should be far more concerned with a more basic theoretical issue that *L'uomo dalla croce* raises. It is not so important to determine whether Rossellini was a convinced fascist ideologue at this time in his career. He was not. Nor is it crucial to ascertain whether Rossellini's lack of political commitment to an antifascist cause at this time reflects a flaw in his personal character. Many would claim it does. Historically, few artists, writers, or musicians could measure up to the kind of ethical standard that judges their works by the degree to which their creators' political or social system approached the benchmark of Western democracy.

The most intriguing question posed by a film such as *L'uomo dalla croce* concerns the relationship between the prewar "fascist" cinema and the postwar "neorealist" cinema. Is this relationship characterized by continuity, evolution, or a sharp and unequivocal break? We must now turn to Rossellini's enduring neorealist classics, *Roma città aperta* and *Paisà*, in search of an answer.

3
Roma città aperta and the Birth of Italian Neorealism

In spite of the many precursors film historians have cited as antecedents of Italian neorealism during the fascist period, and especially during the early 1940s, the birth of Italian neorealism is historically and emotionally linked forever with the astounding international success of Rossellini's portrayal of life in Nazi-occupied Rome between the fall of the fascist regime in September 1943 and its liberation in June of the following year. Unlike the fate of almost all other neorealist films, which seldom had a respectable showing at the box office and were rarely smash hits, *Roma città aperta* was the largest grossing film in Italy during the year it first appeared, and critical reactions in France and the United States, as well as box-office successes there, were equally positive. In addition, the fact that *Paisà* was screened abroad almost simultaneously with *Roma città aperta* helped to create a consciousness among film critics that something new was brewing in Italy (neorealism) and that this new aesthetic phenomenon was largely the creation of an obscure Italian director named Roberto Rossellini.

The film's plot, put together by a team of scriptwriters that included Rossellini, Federico Fellini, and Sergio Amidei, is deceptively simple. A Marxist partisan leader named Giorgio Manfredi who is being hidden from the Germans by a printer named Francesco enlists the assistance of a partisan priest, Don Pietro. The next day, just before Francesco is to be married to his pregnant fiancée, Pina, she is gunned down by the Germans when they arrest Francesco. Manfredi is the object of an intense manhunt by the German Gestapo, led by an evil and effeminate Nazi, Major Bergmann. The major is assisted by his lesbian agent, Ingrid, who uses drugs to obtain information about Manfredi from Marina, a dancer and Manfredi's old girlfriend. The somewhat incredible link between such different figures as Manfredi, Marina, Francesco, and Pina is effected by the fortuitous script

45

Desperate times: breadlines in front of a bakery during the German occupation of Rome. *Source*: Museum of Modern Art Film Stills Archives

invention that depicts Marina as a close friend of Pina's sister. Manfredi, Don Pietro, and an Austrian deserter from the battlefield of Monte Cassino whom the priest has been hiding are all captured by Bergmann after Ingrid induces Marina to betray them in return for drugs and furs. The deserter hangs himself; Manfredi refuses to talk under torture, while Don Pietro looks on in dismay, and dies from the brutal treatment he has received; the next morning, the priest faces a firing squad while the young boys from his parish witness the event.

For a film, such as *Gone with the Wind, Citizen Kane,* or *La dolce vita,* to transcend its status as a work of art and become a social phenomenon that seems to exemplify the cultural atmosphere of its time, a series of fortuitous circumstances and favorable timing are always required. This is true in the case of *Roma città aperta;* the history of the creation of this film reveals a bit of the serendipity that seems to happen only in the movies. However, a popular mythology has grown up around the film that is misleading and, in some aspects, false. A good deal of the mythology surrounding this work is associated with its "realistic" qualities, and as the first important neorealist film, much of what has been written about Italian neorealism has often used the film as a springboard for defining this phenomenon in film history, sometimes with quite confusing results.

Conventional wisdom about *Roma città aperta* emphasizes the film's technical novelties and practically ignores its relationship to the cinema of the fascist period, in which Rossellini received his training. Thus, the legend arose that Rossellini decided to employ "authentic" locations because Cinecittà's studios either were destroyed by bombings or were filled to capacity sheltering refugees. In fact, there are important precedents for on-location shooting during the fascist period that have already been discussed, particularly works by De Robertis and Alessandrini that certainly must have influenced Rossellini. Of course, Rossellini himself in his own prewar fascist trilogy often employs authentic locations (especially in *La nave bianca*). In stressing on-location shooting, early reactions to the film neglected to note that the majority of the film's sequences actually take place in interiors. But even more important, the lack of studios at Cinecittà did not result in the use of "real" interior settings. Rossellini merely constructed four completely conventional interior sets for the most important locations in the film – Don Pietro's sacristy, Gestapo headquarters, the torture room, and the living room where the German officers relax – in a vacant basement of a building on Rome's Via degli Avignonesi. As Federico Fellini has recounted the story, the location of these interiors played a major role in the reception of Italian neorealism abroad, for it was on the same street (number 36) that a celebrated Roman brothel operated by Signora Tina Trabucchi was located. One night while shooting was taking place, an American soldier named

The corrupt Marina, whose relationship with Ingrid, the lesbian assistant to the Gestapo commander, will lead to her betrayal of the Resistance and her lover Manfredi. *Source*: Centro sperimentale di cinematografia Photograph Archives

Rod Geiger, presumably exiting from Signora Trabucchi's establishment, staggered drunkenly across the street and tripped over the electric cables supplying current to Rossellini's crew. Steadied by a solicitous Fellini, Geiger watched the production, became fascinated by the film, and eventually convinced Rossellini to sell him the American rights for only twenty thousand dollars. Even Rossellini's discovery by the man who became his first American producer was a serendipitous affair, the stuff of which myths are made.[1] The documentary quality of the film's photography has always been one of the benchmarks of traditional definitions of neorealism. Here, conventional wisdom has always been closer to the mark. To be sure, the grainy character of the film (as well as the few brief segments of actual documentary footage inserted by the editor into the fictional story) certainly reminded viewers who saw the film when it was first released of the kinds of pictures they associated with the newsreels. The scarcity of film stock forced Rossellini to buy 35-millimeter film in bits and pieces on the black market, causing him to use stock of different quality and provenance. In addition, the variance in the lighting was often striking; Rome was still suffering from the deprivations of the war, and the electric current experienced drastic and unexpected fluctuations. But even in this regard, the facile association of the film's photographic style with realism cannot always be sustained. Perhaps it is more accurate to state that in 1945, such a photographic style seemed realistic because audiences associated black-and-white film photography with "real" events. Today, however, most audiences associate realism with live television broadcasts in color. Few contemporary audiences will be struck by the realism of the photography in the Rossellini film. On the contrary, the perspective of almost half a century reveals clear expressionistic elements in some of the photography and the lighting in crucial sequences, such as the torture scene.[2] The definition of the so-called photographic realism in *Roma città aperta* thus depends in some measure on our personal experience and knowledge of cinematic history. Much the same may be said of the post-synchronization of its sound track. Because of a lack of funds, Rossellini was obliged to shoot without direct sound (developing silent footage cost some sixty lire per meter, whereas developing synchronized footage cost hundreds of lire more).[3] Another result of the financial situation was Rossellini's avoidance of daily rushes, another cost-cutting measure. Although it is true that the lack of sound during shooting gave the director more freedom of movement with his camera, which many traditional critics see as a factor in the film's heightened realism, dubbed sound in a film studio certainly does not create a direct link to the world "out there," which was supposed to be the neorealist's aesthetic goal. Post-synchronization of sound

48

became almost the norm in Italy for several decades as the result of neorealist practice, and it has been only recently that some directors, such as Bernardo Bertolucci, have moved back toward the international commercial market and synchronized sound. It is difficult to maintain that post-synchronization is realistic. In fact, both Pasolini and Fellini, to mention only two Italian directors who have always dubbed their sound tracks, have declared that they do so precisely to avoid any hint of naturalism or realism in their works. However, in dubbing the sound after the shooting, Rossellini was able to heighten the authenticity of the sound track by having his Germans speak German and his Italians speak Italian, something that must surely have struck many American viewers as realistic when Hollywood's commercial cinema often handled this problem quite differently – by having foreigners speak either a kind of Oxford English or a heavily accented English to distinguish them from the Americans.

Perhaps the most persuasive of the many stylistic elements traditional definitions cite as typical of Italian neorealism is a reliance upon nonprofessional actors. As we have seen in our survey of Italian cinema during the fascist period, however, there was nothing original in this. Perhaps it would be more precise to say that rarely have nonprofessional actors been used so skillfully as they were by Rossellini in *Paisà*, De Sica in *Ladri di biciclette* (*The Bicycle Thief*, 1948), or Visconti in *La terra trema* (*The Earth Trembles*, 1948). But this exploitation of nonprofessional actors for particular aesthetic effects is totally absent from *Roma città aperta*. The entire cast of the film had extensive experience in the entertainment world. Aldo Fabrizi (Don Pietro) and Anna Magnani (Pina), both of whom were catapulted to international fame with the success of the film, had extensive experience in the entertainment business, not only in the music hall form of *avanspettacolo* entertainment roughly equivalent to America's vaudeville, but also in film roles together, where the particular chemistry of their artistic personalities had already achieved commercial success in Mario Bonard's comic film *Campo de' fiori* (*Campo de' Fiori Square*, 1943). Marcello Pagliero (Manfredi) had already directed a film of his own. Harry Feist (Major Bergmann) was a dancer, as was Maria Michi (Marina), who probably landed her part not because she had been working as an usher at the Barberini Cinema but, instead, because she was scriptwriter Sergio Amidei's mistress. Even minor roles, such as those played by Nando Bruno (the sacristan) and Edoardo Passarelli (the policeman), were filled by actors who came from the variety hall. Rather than basing his film on nonprofessional acting performances, Rossellini relied upon the consummate skills of seasoned professionals, but he cast his troupe in unaccustomed roles, placing figures normally associated with comic roles in situations that would call for tragic or tragicomic actions.[4]

The hybrid system of casting marking Rossellini's production offers an insight into the director's aesthetic intentions, for "hybrid" style might well be taken as the most appropriate description of Rossellini's manner, following the dictionary definition of the term that explains the word with synonyms such as "medley," "mixture," or "combination." *Roma città aperta* does not completely abandon or reject traditional cinematic style or generic conventions and replace them with an absolutely original neorealist style or neorealist cinematic conventions of Rossellini's invention. For example, Rossellini's editing is, as Brunette has pointed out, for the most part " 'classic' – that is, illusionist, meant to be as invisible as the traditional Hollywood variety" because it serves primarily to underscore the narrative line and to increase emotional involvement.[5] There is very little of the montage we associate with Eisenstein and that Rossellini employed so skillfully in *La nave bianca,* nor are there many extremely long takes, the future direction of Rossellini's cinema, hints of which can be detected in *L'uomo dalla croce.* Instead, Rossellini introduces a number of novel elements into a conventional context, and their power depends precisely upon the viewer's interpreting them against the backdrop of traditional cinematic practice. Moreover, the ideological and ethical message of the film is more than a hybrid and might best be described as a philosophical compromise wherein views of extremely different political groups are telescoped into the small cast of characters in the film in an uneasy synthesis that would not endure for long in the turbulent world of Italian domestic politics. Perhaps Rossellini's greatest achievement in this film was to fuse the narrative structure of his hybrid creation with the ideological compromise in the film's script so that each complemented the other harmoniously, as our discussion of the film will demonstrate.

Rossellini's portrayal of Italian life under German occupation reflects a stark juxtaposition of good (the Resistance forces) and evil (the perverted Nazis and their much less offensive Italian allies) that reminds the viewer of the ideological world of *L'uomo dalla croce,* where Bolsheviks were identified with barbarism and Italians were defending Western civilization. Now the Nazis replace the Bolsheviks, but unlike that earlier film (where Sergei and Irina were clearly sympathetic figures), the Nazis embody unmitigated evil with no redeeming virtues whatsoever. Rossellini treats the most important German figures as he had depicted Fyodor earlier. It is not enough for him that Bergmann is a moral monster. He is also portrayed as an effeminate homosexual, and his assistant Ingrid is a viper-like lesbian

Neorealist cheesecake: Manfredi's girlfriend, Marina, in her negligee. *Source*: Museum of Modern Art Film Stills Archives

who seduces Marina with drugs and furs to obtain information about Manfredi. The tone of the work is thus far more indebted to Rossellini's message of Christian humanism than to any programmatic attempt at cinematic realism. The positive characters who fight the Nazis are joined by their belief in what Francesco calls an impending "springtime" in Italy and a better tomorrow. Pina, Francesco, Don Pietro, and Manfredi are all united by this faith in a brighter future, while Marina and Pina's sister Lauretta are mesmerized by the superficial values of café society and the consumer goods proffered by the Germans with whom they associate. Marina is corrupted not because of Ingrid's blandishments but, rather, because she lacks faith in herself and, therefore, is incapable of loving others. Marxists and Christians alike adhere to Rossellini's Christian credo best embodied in Don Pietro's last words before he faces a firing squad: "Oh, it's not hard to die well. It's hard to live well."[6] In fact, as a detailed analysis of the torture sequence reveals, the iconography of Manfredi's death associates him with the crucified Christ.

Rossellini effects a kind of "historical compromise" between Catholicism and Marxism within the partisan ranks, but this should in no way be construed as a falsification of the historical facts. Italian Communists have done their best to picture the anti-Nazi Resistance as a purely communist phenomenon, but the truth is much more complicated, with contributions coming from all segments of Italian society, including perhaps the most significant from members of the royal armed forces and the police, whose actions are usually only grudgingly recognized by both the Catholic and the Marxist elements within the Resistance.

The script for *Roma città aperta* incorporates these very real ideological and historical tensions that, in turn, embody authentic forces within the fabric of Italian society. The fact that the script was so crucial to the making of the film also undercuts another of the myths about Italian neorealism and Rossellini's stylistic contribution to it – that of improvisation. There was little about the film that was not argued out and written over and over again, and the slow evolution of the script says a great deal about the ideological perspectives of the various scriptwriters involved. Rossellini's original idea, entitled *Storie di ieri (Stories of Yesterday)*, was to treat the events leading to the execution on 4 April 1944 of Don Giuseppe Morosini, a Catholic priest active in the Resistance. Before speaking to Rossellini about this particular idea, Sergio Amidei, an extremely talented scriptwriter of well-known communist sympathies, had begun another script on the black market. After discussing the two concepts, the two men decided to include Amidei's material in a new episodic film about the Nazi occupation of Rome. Subsequently, a Neapolitan journalist named Alberto Consiglio suggested a story about a partisan priest named Don Pappagallo, and after a producer was found, Consiglio (who was never credited for his work) combined his fictitious character with Don Morosini to produce the outline of what finally became Don Pietro. Before the liberation, Amidei had read about another striking incident, the savage machine-gunning of a pregnant woman in Viale Giulio Cesare as she ran after her husband, arrested during one of the German dragnets. This figure evolved into Pina, and Pina's death would become the single most dramatic moment of the film. It was apparently Amidei who insisted upon the addition to the script of a Marxist partisan, Manfredi, to ensure, at least to his satisfaction, that there would be one model hero reflecting his own ideological position. All accounts of the production of the film unanimously agree that the writer who shaped the figure of the priest in the final script was none other than Federico Fellini, who was a close friend of Aldo Fabrizi. Rossellini first met Fellini when he approached Fellini to ask him to convince his friend Fabrizi to take the role of Don Pietro. Fellini had begun his career as a cartoonist and gag writer with the Roman humor magazine *Marc'Aurelio,* and after an apprenticeship with the magazine, he had turned (as so many other writers connected with it did) to scriptwriting for the cinema, particularly film comedies. Fabrizi's performance, requiring an almost perfect balance between comic timing and serious tragic dignity, owes a great deal to Fellini's contributions to the script. And it was definitely Fellini's inspiration to insert the frying-pan gag into the action, a slapstick routine typical of his writing for earlier comic films. It was a mark of Rossellini's intelligence that he succeeded in blending the talents of two completely different men within a single screenplay: the apolitical Fellini, who had comic wit and a sure awareness of how to manipulate the audience's emotions, and the leftist intellectual Amidei, who had a sounder understanding of how to set individual incidents within a broader political context. When Rossellini accepted Fellini's comic interpretation of Don Pietro and, in the final editing, juxtaposed this sequence of hilarious slapstick comedy from the variety theater with the moment of darkest pathos in the film – the sequence in which Pina is killed – the team of scriptwriters and director succeeded in producing one of the most moving moments in the history of the cinema.

Rossellini never avoids the hints of tension between the two forces within the Resistance that would be locked in a struggle for power in postwar Italy that has continued to this day. Manfredi, for example, expresses mild disapproval of Pina's religious marriage, but she notes that it is better to be married by a partisan priest than by a Fascist official at city hall. In another scene, a leftist printer pointedly tells Don Pietro that everyone is not lucky enough to be able to hide in a monastery. Even more significant in this regard are the proposals that Major Bergmann makes to both Don Pietro and Manfredi after he has captured them both. To Manfredi, he offers to spare the members of his party if he betrays the more conservative, Catholic members of the Resistance, but Manfredi rejects his proposal by spitting on him, an action of defiance that results in his renewed torture and eventual death. To Don Pietro, Bergmann argues persuasively that the Communists are the sworn enemies of the church, who will destroy all organized religion if they take power. Don Pietro replies that all men who fight for justice and liberty walk in the pathways of the Lord.

As befits a film whose main actors came from the music hall theater and film comedy, *Roma città aperta* contains a great deal of authentic humor, but the humor is placed within a profoundly tragicomic vision of life that juxtaposes melodramatic moments or instances of comic relief and dark humor to the most tragic of human experiences that reconstruct a moment in recent Italian history. The church, and Don Pietro in particular, are the object of much of this humor.[7] When the sexton, Agostino, says he cannot loot a bakery because he works for the church, Pina sarcastically informs him he will have to eat his cake in Paradise. When Don Pietro visits a religious shop over Resistance headquarters, he is offended by the proximity

Neorealist comedy: the partisan priest turns his eyes away from a nude statue standing too close to a statue of a saint. *Source*: Museum of Modern Art Film Stills Archives

of a statue of Saint Rocco and one of a nude woman; first he turns the nude around (giving the saint a beautiful view of the woman's backside), and then after reconsidering the problem, he decides that the saint should not be subjected to temptation and turns his face away from the nude as well! When Fascist soldiers arrive to search the workers' apartments on Via Casilina to look for concealed partisans, Manfredi and others manage to escape because the Italian troops are preoccupied with trying to peer up the skirts of the women on the staircase. It is important to note that these troops are Italians, pictured throughout the film as likable but bumbling and ineffectual clowns, in contrast to the superefficient Germans, who would never act in such an unmilitary and undisciplined manner. This generally comic and sympathetic portrait of Italian officials continues when a tolerant Italian policeman observes Pina and other women looting a bakery. Rather than doing his duty, the man sadly remarks he wishes he were not in uniform so that he could join them. The film's humor takes on a decidedly somber and negative tone when it is directed at the Germans. As German soldiers enter a restaurant where Manfredi is eating, we immediately fear that he is about to be arrested, but this suspense is alleviated by our discovery that the Germans have only come to butcher a live lamb and to eat it, and our fear (as well as Manfredi's) is dissolved by the humorous quip of the restaurant owner, Flavio – he says he forgot that Germans were specialists in butchering!

The entire film revolves around Rossellini's adept shifting of perspectives from a comic to a tragic tone, and nowhere is this more evident than in the film's most famous sequences, involving the search of Pina's apartment building and her subsequent death as she races after Francesco being carried away in a truck. The event occurs on the day of their wedding; thus, the promise of a new springtime in Italy that Francesco described to Pina earlier will end in tragedy and death. But this tragedy is introduced by a slapstick comic scene worthy of the best vaudevillian traditions. As the Germans and the Italian troops under their command inspect the building, Don Pietro and Marcello (Pina's son, now dressed as an altar boy) arrive at the apartment complex supposedly to give the last rites to Pina's father, but actually to locate and conceal weapons and bombs kept in the building by one of

Neorealist comedy: Rossellini's camera captures the point of view of the Italian soldiers, who are preoccupied with looking up the skirts of the women in the apartment building rather than capturing the antifascist Resistance members. *Source*: Museum of Modern Art Film Stills Archives

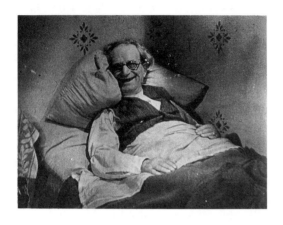

The grandfather smiles in bed, thinking about the cake he will eat at Pina's wedding. *Source*: Museum of Modern Art Film Stills Archives

Marcello's friends, a crippled young man named appropriately Romoletto ("Little Romulus"). Romoletto represents a mirror image of the partisans but in a comic key, and his earlier appearances in the film generate laughter when he repeats Marxist political slogans without really understanding their significance. In spite of Rossellini's often-cited aversion to dramatic editing, a feature of his later, mature style that will be discussed in subsequent chapters, here he skillfully builds suspense as he cuts back and forth between the priest's search for the weapons and his subsequent descent to the dying man's room, on the one hand, and the menacing ascent of the suspicious Fascist officer and his troops, on the other. When the soldiers finally enter the room, Don Pietro can be seen peacefully administering the last rites to Pina's father, who is wearing a beatific smile, with Marcello at his side. Only after the danger is passed and the priest frantically attempts to revive the moribund sleeper do we understand that to calm the old man (who was

Romoletto, the leader of the children who mimic their elders in opposing the Germans. *Source*: Museum of Modern Art Film Stills Archives

Fellini's comic gag: Don Pietro just after he has hit the grandfather on the head with a frying pan to silence him while Fascist troops search the apartment for arms. *Source*: Museum of Modern Art Film Stills Archives

terrified when he awoke and saw a priest ready to administer the last rites to him), Don Pietro had knocked the man unconscious with a frying pan, which now reveals a huge dent in it when examined by Marcello. The contraband weapons were hidden underneath the old man's bed only a moment before the arrival of the Fascist soldiers.

Comic gags disappear thereafter, for in defiance of the soldiers around her, Pina runs after the truck carrying Francesco. Immediately prior to the shooting that ends her life, Rossellini's camera shifts to the interior of the truck to capture the scene from Francesco's point of view, and the fact that we share it increases the dramatic impact of the scene. We hear a loud burst of machine-gun fire, Marcello races toward his mother screaming, and Pina is shown lying in the street, her face turned in the agony of death and her right leg bared to a garter belt, an image underlining the obscenity of her untimely demise. In the next sequence, and completely without rhetorical or sentimental emphasis of any kind, Francesco's truck is ambushed by partisans in one of the very few exterior sequences Rossellini employs in the film. As Francesco escapes, we suddenly realize that Pina's death was completely meaningless, like so many occurrences in wartime.

The scenes situated at Gestapo headquarters in Via Tasso are justly considered among the most moving of the entire film, and they, too, are constructed around the juxtaposition of different moods and cinematic techniques.[8] And in these sequences, contrary to the traditional belief that sets are of little importance in neorealist films, the very structure of the set

Pina races after Francesco, who has been arrested by the Germans; the camera captures the scene just before her death from Francesco's perspective within the moving truck. *Source*: Centro sperimentale di cinematografia Photograph Archives

The obscenity of Pina's sudden and useless death; her young son cries over her body. *Source*: Museum of Modern Art Film Stills Archives

58

Major Bergmann opening the door of his office so that Don Pietro can see Manfredi being prepared for torture. *Source*: Museum of Modern Art Film Stills Archives

itself heightens Rossellini's drama. From the central office in which Bergmann interrogates his prisoners, there are two doors opening out onto entirely different worlds. One door leads into a torture chamber inhabited by ghoulish Nazis whose fingers are stained with the blood of their victims and who nonchalantly and indifferently light their cigarettes with the same blowtorch with which they scorch Manfredi's chest. The other plunges us into a completely different, decadent atmosphere where German officers play cards, drink brandy or champagne, listen to piano music, and chat pleasantly, oblivious to the human suffering on the other side of the wall.

Only Bergmann moves effortlessly between these three different locations, and his physical movements between them, viewed most often from Don Pietro's perspective, who remains in the central room and peers through each door, accentuate the emotional and moral distance between the two individuals. Ironically, while we are privileged to see every little detail of the horrible drama that is unfolding, Don Pietro's spectacles have been broken during his capture, and the point-of-view shots nominally from his perspective are much clearer than if he had actually viewed them himself.

Manfredi's torture is one of the most horrifying scenes in the history of filmmaking, and yet, Rossellini achieves an enormously emotional impact upon his audience without ever showing the viewer the actual events of his torture. Instead, we see detailed close-ups of the anguished reactions of a myopic Don Pietro who can hardly see the scene himself. Voice-overs convey the screams from the other room, and like Don Pietro without his glasses, we experience the torture of Manfredi through the power of our imagination. Even in this scene tragedy mixes with black humor. While Manfredi's agony moves the priest to tears, a German soldier quietly sharpens his pencil and awaits Bergmann's orders. When Manfredi dies, without revealing the names of his compatriots, Rossellini frames this Communist partisan leader as if he were photographing the crucified Christ, employing the traditional iconography familiar to us all from numerous works of art. The final touch to this picture of moral degradation is provided by a drunken Marina, who strolls from the salon where Ingrid is entertaining her, unaware that the ex-lover she has betrayed is being tortured to death in the next room. She is draped in the luxurious fur coat that she has received as her reward, but as she peers into the room with Hartmann and sees Manfredi, she screams and faints. Ingrid's only reaction is to scold Bergmann for his failure, reminding him that she did not think it would be easy to break Manfredi and then coolly picking up the coat Marina has dropped, with the callous remark: "For the next time."[9]

During Manfredi's torment, Rossellini introduces the viewer to another German officer, Major Hartmann, who listens to the piano with Bergmann and Ingrid in the adjacent salon. There, Bergmann declares to Hartmann that the Germans are a master race and that the Italian under interrogation would eventually betray his cause. If he did not, then Italians would not be inferior to Germans and the war to defend the master race would have no meaning. Hartmann, reckless with too much liquor, argues with Bergmann, telling him that during World War I, the Germans supposed that the people they fought were lesser men, and yet, at that time French patriots died under torture without giving in to their interrogators. Here, at long last, Rossellini seems to be saying, is a German with a conscience. However, the next morning after Manfredi's death, when Don Pietro is sentenced to die by a firing squad, it is the same Major Hartmann, now sober, who commands the Italian troops assigned to perform this gruesome task. And when the superstitious young Italian draftees refuse to shoot a priest (yet another instance where Rossellini portrays Italians as likable but ineffectual and nonpolitical), it is Hartmann who delivers the coup de grâce with his pistol with little hesitation and certainly with none of the self-doubt that characterized him when he was drunk. In Rossellini's Manichaean moral universe, it seems a German can have a conscience only when intoxicated.

After having manipulated the viewer's emotions throughout the film with

As he is being tortured, Manfredi is captured by Rossellini's camera in a pose reminiscent of the crucified Christ. *Source*: Centro sperimentale di cinematografia Photograph Archives

Not realizing that Manfredi is being tortured in a nearby room, Marina lounges in the salon with her lover Ingrid, making pleasant conversation with Major Bergmann, the Gestapo commander. *Source*: Centro sperimentale di cinematografia Photograph Archives

such skill, Rossellini does not conclude his film on a completely negative note. Not only does the torture scene contain the iconography traditionally associated with the crucified Christ, but the tone of the last sequence is triumphantly associated with the concept of Christian resurrection and rebirth. Romoletto, Marcello, and the other children observe Don Pietro's execution (no adult witnesses are present besides the soldiers), and as they leave the scene, Rossellini pans after them, Italy's future, placing the children against the backdrop of the dome of St. Peter's Cathedral. Passing from an image of tragic despair to another full of promise for the "springtime in Italy" Francesco foretold earlier in the film, Rossellini creates a vision of hope with this first of many symbolic images associated with children that characterize so many of the neorealist classics.

It should be clear from this analysis of *Roma città aperta* that Rossellini's film succeeds precisely because it combines a number of new stylistic elements not normally associated with commercial cinema with what one critical interpretation labels "bourgeois illusionist cinema," a style reflecting

> a total and unquestioning mastery of a system of representation built up by bourgeois film culture from D. W. Griffith on. It is a system of representation whose fundamental intent is to make the audience suspend its disbelief, and enter the world of the film *as if* it were the real world; the audience is encouraged to read the time and space of the film's actions as homogenous, unified, 'real': the emphasis on 'reality' at the structural level leads to a masking of the process of production of meaning.[10]

The negative tone of this particular interpretation has been echoed by other critics who have embraced a modernist aesthetic associated in the theater with Bertolt Brecht and in the cinema with Jean-Luc Godard and film theorists influenced by both Brecht and Godard. When Rossellini's neorealist works first appeared, he was seen virtually as the creator of an entirely new realistic aesthetic. Currently, in some critical circles, his reliance upon traditional devices of melodrama – identification with the film's central characters, manipulation of the audience's emotional responses to dramatic situations, an edifying conclusion offering hope of improvement, the use of children to evoke a sentimental response in the viewer – has been cited as proof that Rossellini and neorealism in general were politically conservative, if not reactionary, and that little of any consequence was achieved by what has traditionally been defined as a revolution in the history of the cinema with the critical triumphs of Rossellini, De Sica, and Visconti (not to mention a host of lesser figures).[11]

The truth lies somewhere between these two extreme critical positions. The early praise of Rossellini for creating an entirely new film aesthetic can certainly not be sustained with *Roma città aperta* as the test case. As we shall see in the next chapter, an argument for Rossellini's originality can more easily be made with *Paisà*. Rossellini's innovations in the first part of his neorealist trilogy lie in his unique understanding of how the boundaries of traditional cinematic narrative could be stretched in a direction that would bear fruit in his subsequent works. But to say that early assessments of this film were overblown is not to admit the validity of the strictures brought against Rossellini of late – that he failed to adopt a modernist aesthetic similar to one espoused by Brecht or Godard and that he did not aim to change society with his films. To deny the evident emotional power of a masterpiece such as *Roma città aperta* on the grounds that it breaks a set of modernist rules few writers in the history of literature and even fewer directors in the history of the cinema would accept reflects the kind of politically correct thinking that has become part of so much contemporary academic writing. Neither exaggerating Rossellini's originality in *Roma città aperta* nor belittling the emotional impact of what must be defined as a hybrid brand of cinema combining the codes of the traditional narrative cinema with some bold innovations does justice to the creative force that emerges in Rossellini's masterpiece and almost unassisted moves Italian cinema in a different direction for the next decade.

4
Paisà and
the Rejection
of Traditional
Narrative Cinema

Although a far less popular work than *Roma città aperta*, it is *Paisà* that moves Rossellini's narrative farthest from traditional cinematic patterns associated with the Hollywood melodrama toward an original and revolutionary style.[1] The plot of *Paisà* unfolds in six brief stories that are separate episodes with completely different protagonists in each. André Bazin has quite rightly compared the film to a collection of American short stories.[2] The six episodes are shaped by recent Italian history; chronologically and geographically they follow the path taken by the Allied invasion of Italy. In each episode, Italians and their American liberators meet and interact with varying degrees of familiarity and human warmth. The film thus passes through six locations, moving step by step from the Allied invasion of Italy beginning in Sicily, to liberated Naples, to Rome six months after the city's liberation, to Florence while the struggle between the last Fascist holdouts and partisans still continues for control of the city, to a monastery in the Apennines visited by three American chaplains, and finally to the Po River Valley, where Italian partisans and their Allied advisers are captured by the Germans shortly before the war ended in Italy in 1945. Originally, the film was to have been called *Sette americani (Seven Americans)* and was to have included seven episodes. Although the original manuscript of the final draft of the script no longer exists, a recent discovery of various undated draft copies of script and scenario materials in the Cinémathèque française in Paris reveals that a number of changes were made in the script before Rossellini settled upon the six episodes in the completed work. These documents include two episodes that were never shot: one called "La nurse" ("The Nurse") about an American nurse in Naples killed during a bombing raid; another called "Il prigioniero" ("The Prisoner"), set in the hills around Rome before the liberation of the city, where a German patrol encounters a small group of Americans in jeeps and kills an Italian peasant. In addition, variants of the fifth and sixth episodes in the Apennine monastery and the Po Valley have also been found. These are earlier versions of stories written by Sergio Amidei that were later changed significantly. The monastery sequence, as we shall see later, was modified substantially by Federico Fellini, and it appears that the suggestions of the partisans themselves in recounting their personal adventures during the Resistance shaped the final version of the last sequence in the Po Valley.

Unlike *Roma città aperta*, which may legitimately be identified with the birth of neorealism but which has numerous, very obvious ties to traditional prewar melodrama in both Italy and Hollywood, *Paisà* remains much closer to the spirit of the newsreel documentary. Its episodic organization and accurate chronology for the most part respect the history of the events portrayed in the film. Many of the generic conventions of newsreels, with which all film audiences were familiar during the 1940s in both Italy and the United States, are also present in the film. There is an authoritative voice-over that introduces each episode with reliable information about the basic facts of the events to be represented. As each episode begins, the voice-over is supplemented by a map showing troop movements. More important, in each episode, actual newsreel footage is combined with the invented narrative Rossellini shot in such a way that "fact" and "fiction" blend together in a seamless whole, and the editing is performed in such a manner that it is extremely difficult at first glance to distinguish between the two kinds of footage. The quality of the lighting and the photography reinforce this feeling of authenticity – that is, the kind of authenticity one would expect from a newsreel of the 1940s, not what we have come to expect from live television coverage by satellite in color. But like live television coverage, Rossellini manages to re-create the sense of actuality and immediacy of subject matter that we associate with documentary newsreels.

Traditional definitions of Italian neorealism have always stressed its effective use of nonprofessional actors and actual, nonstudio locations. We have already seen how *Roma città aperta* does not follow this convention; almost all the protagonists were played by actors with extensive theatrical experience, and the most important interior locations were constructed sets. In *Paisà* Rossellini remains far closer to traditional definitions of neorealism. This is evident first of all in the physical settings that encompass the film's action. The rubble of a bombed-out Naples in the second episode, for instance, speaks far more eloquently of the misery that followed the liberation of that city than any reconstructed movie set probably could. The sequence in the Po Valley, shot among the shallow inlets and canals lined with reeds and aquatic plants, represents one of the most intelligent uses of an outside location in all of neorealist cinema. As André Bazin so aptly put it, by keeping his camera low and never letting it rise above the height of a crouched person, Rossellini reproduces "the exact equivalent, under conditions imposed by the screen, of the inner feeling men experience who are living between the sky and the water and whose lives are at the mercy of an infinitesimal shift of angle in relation to the horizon."[3] In another textbook example of selecting neorealist locations, Rossellini and Fellini arranged to film bar scenes (where the American soldiers meet Italian prostitutes) for this third Roman sequence in one of the city's best known dives, employing about twenty actual GIs and about thirty *"segnorine"* (prostitutes) who, like the female protagonist in the episode, were all forced into a life on the streets as a result of the economic hardships in the aftermath of the war. Filming at the precise physical location of his fictional story greatly enhanced the credibility of Rossellini's work. Elements such as these comply with the classic neorealist dictum of taking the camera out into the streets to photograph reality. But other locations have been so artfully contrived that they have succeeded in deceiving critics and viewers of the film for years. One recent and comprehensive study of Rossellini's work, for example, claimed that only in the monastery sequence does the director "cheat,"[4] because he filmed this segment in Maiori along the Amalfi coast rather than in the Apennine mountains between Florence and Bologna. However, there are numerous other examples of artificially reproduced locations in the film. The Sicilian episode, for instance, is not shot near Catania in Sicily but on the same coastline near Amalfi where the fifth sequence was filmed.[5] And when American tanks arrive to liberate Rome, the scene is actually shot in Livorno rather than in the capital city because only there were American tanks available for use in the scene.[6] Many of the interior locations supposedly shot in Florence for the fourth sequence were actually done in Rome on Via Lutezia near the home of the aunt of Giulietta Masina, Fellini's wife.

Rossellini's choice of locations combines authentic places that reveal the local color of precise geographical spots with artfully contrived locations that are so similar to the real thing that they have succeeded in fooling the critics for years. His hybrid technique of blending actual documentary footage with footage shot to look as if it were documentary and of intermingling authentic locations with re-created locations that can hardly be distinguished

66

Fred's tank stops on a Roman street outside Francesca's home during the liberation of the city (a scene actually filmed in Livorno). *Source*: Museum of Modern Art Film Stills Archives

from the authentic is continued in the selection of the actors who portray the protagonists of this vast historical drama played out over the entire Italian peninsula. Few viewers of *Paisà* have failed to be impressed by the incredibly moving performances of a number of nonprofessional actors in the film. Rossellini himself has assisted in the creation of a mythology about his nonprofessional actors by describing how he would put his cameraman in the middle of a town square where he planned to shoot and would wait for the curious to gather, from whom he selected faces that interested him.[7] In the first Sicilian sequence, for example, the young Italian girl playing Carmela (Carmela Sazio) was discovered by Rossellini from his moving automobile as she was carrying water on her head in a small town near Naples,[8] and Robert Van Loon, her American counterpart playing Joe from Jersey, was a real GI. The Neapolitan street urchin, Pasquale, was, of course, not a professional actor, nor were the Franciscan monks of the monastery sequence and many of the partisans in Florence and the Po Valley. In fact, in both of the partisan sequences Rossellini questioned those who had actually lived the events he was about to film in order to modify his script, and in the final sequence, Cigolani was an authentic partisan leader who played himself in the film. But it is completely inaccurate to explain the film's realistic feel solely because of the presence of its nonprofessional actors. On the contrary, the well-documented history of the film's production provides ample proof that Rossellini and his producer were quite anxious to have American actors in the cast. Fellini has often recounted the amusing story of how Rod Geiger promised Rossellini a number of major Hollywood stars, including Gregory Peck, Lana Turner, and Paul Robeson, only to disappoint them when he arrived in Naples on a transatlantic steamer with a series of unknowns in tow: Dots Johnson (an American soldier in the Naples sequence), Gar Moore (the American tanker in the Rome sequence), Harriet White (the nurse in love with the Florentine partisan Lupo), Bill Tubbs (the Catholic chaplain, Bill Martin), and Dale Edmonds (Dale, the American liaison officer with the Po Valley partisans).[9] Even though Rod Geiger contests Fellini's entertaining description of the arrival of this troupe of unknown actors, his own version of the story also underlines the interest Rossellini had in bringing famous Hollywood actors to Italy to work on the film.[10]

These Americans were certainly not stars, but they were nevertheless professionals with extensive theatrical experience in the United States. And it is instructive to note that in each episode containing large numbers of nonprofessional actors, usually in minor roles, the crucial parts in each sequence are masterfully portrayed by these professionals. Far more important to the successful completion of the film and to its believable acting was the interplay between screenwriters, director, and actors (both professional and nonprofessional). As the assistant director Massimo Mida has pointed out, the script was constantly modified to suit the various personalities involved in each scene. Thus, in the Naples sequence, the script took shape only after the young street urchin (a nonprofessional) and the imported American black actor Dots Johnson had met each other and developed a personal chemistry between their very different personalities.[11] Something similar must have occurred in the fifth sequence, in the monastery, where three Allied chaplains visit a group of secluded Franciscan monks. The Catholic chaplain was played by a professional actor (Tubbs), but the Protestant chaplain was an actual army chaplain, and the Jewish rabbi was portrayed by an actual army rabbi's assistant.[12] In almost every instance where critics have traditionally been tempted to explain the film's greatness by its reliance upon "real" sets, actors, or situations, upon closer examination we shall discover that there is a far more complex relationship between the technical means Rossellini and his troupe employed and the "reality" they filmed. And the complexity invariably consists in Rossellini's magical combination of elements from the society around him (actual locations, real people, true stories) with the artifice of the traditional cinema (professional actors, re-created sets, invented stories).

68

Although much of the critical literature devoted to *Paisà* has emphasized its style and its reflection of the socioeconomic conditions in Italy during the Allied invasion of the country, Rossellini's subject is not merely a realistic view of this historical event. Instead, he focuses on a far more philosophical theme: the interaction and enrichment of two quite alien cultures, Italian and American. The progressive stages in this mutual encounter, portrayed in six vignettes, are set against the backdrop of the Italian landscape, which itself assumes a role as major protagonist. Central to Rossellini's treatment of the meeting of two different worlds is the problem of communication. At first, it is merely a linguistic problem, as representatives of the two countries try to comprehend each other's language, with results that sometimes prove to be tragic when such attempts inevitably break down or become confused. But more important than the problem of linguistic communication is the question of empathy and antipathy between the two different countries and the individuals who represent them. The film's title draws attention to this central theme. *Paisà* is the colloquial form of the word *paisano,* which in Italian means "countryman," "neighbor," "kinsman," even "friend." It was typically used by Italians and American soldiers as a friendly greeting, and the implications of its deeper human significance provide the basis for Rossellini's entire film. The sense of kinship that springs up between people from vastly different ethnic, religious, economic, and political backgrounds in the film also reflects the message of Christian humanism that was at the heart of *Roma città aperta* and would inspire much of Rossellini's early work.

As the film opens in Sicily, the possibilities of empathy between Italians and Americans seem slight. The Sicilians are naturally suspicious of the GIs who are invading their island, even though they are also liberating them from a fascist dictatorship. Rossellini is careful not to portray any of the Sicilians as diehard Fascists, but there is at least one local citizen who mistakes the GIs for Germans and greets them cheerfully; later, he counsels his neighbors not to trust the Americans, even when they learn that one of the soldiers from the States has relatives in the nearby town of Gela. The Americans, of course, are justly suspicious of the intentions of the Italians (or the "Eyeties," as they call them), because Italy and Germany are still allies at this point and Mussolini's government has not yet fallen. One of the townspeople, a young girl named Carmela, nevertheless volunteers to guide a company of American soldiers through a minefield. Carmela leads the soldiers to an old castle or fortress with a tower, as well as a trapdoor and a basement. It seems deserted, but the casual remarks by two of the soldiers remind us that danger is lurking everywhere:

Joe from Jersey speaking with Carmela in the Sicilian sequence just before he is shot by the German sniper. *Source*: Museum of Modern Art Film Stills Archives

SERGEANT: ...Some joint! Hey, Junior, remember Frankenstein? This reminds me of the old mill there!
JUNIOR: Ha ha! It does, now that you mention it. What a place for a murder![13]

The dark, murky atmosphere of the scene is further increased by the fact that Rossellini, for the most part, employs expressionistic lighting in the fortress as if to emphasize the link between the location and the genre of the American horror film. The foreboding ambience of the entrance into the fortress, a perfect place for a murder, is heightened when the sergeant remarks that the place is "as dark as a graveyard" but becomes angry when one of his men flicks the ubiquitous Zippo lighter to improve his vision: "Put that light out, you damn fool! Do you want to get us all killed?"[14] Up to this point, we have yet to see any Germans in the film. But with Rossellini's subtle hints in the dialogue, as well as the expressionist lighting, we are being prepared for something horrible.

Even though the confrontation with the Germans might well be the next logical step in a traditional narrative, the squad goes off on patrol while the camera remains with Carmela and Joe from Jersey, who has been assigned the task of guarding the girl in case she has betrayed the men (as yet, there is no complete trust of the Italians). From this point on, Rossellini's focus shifts to the theme of communication. By his own testimony, Joe from Jersey only understands a few words of what he takes to be Italian: *paisan, spaghetti, bambina, mangiare, tout de suite, c'est la guerre,* and, now that he has met the Sicilian girl, the name *Carmela*. Language proves inadequate to foster their communication. As they witness the appearance of a shooting star, Joe pronounces the words in English, Carmela repeats the meaning in Italian (*stella cadente*), but Joe corrects her by pronouncing the English words once again, demonstrating that he has not understood Carmela. Carmela does the same thing when she confuses the English word "home" with the Italian word *come* ("what"). In order to make himself understood, Joe takes out a picture from his wallet that shows his parents with his brother and sister. Carmela reacts jealously, taking his sister for his girl-friend, and when Joe tries to explain that it is his sister, he forgets the sergeant's warning about showing any lights from the fortress tower and flicks his lighter on, bringing the photograph closer to his face. Joe suddenly drops the lighter and falls to the floor in slow motion, and immediately afterward we see a German soldier in close-up. Not only does Joe die during an unusual slow-motion shot, a technique employed infrequently by Rossellini, but the conversation between Joe and Carmela is rendered by two takes that differ from the preceding shots in their extreme length.[15] Rossellini's effective use of the long take here demonstrates his mastery of a technique that was to characterize his introspective films of the 1950s.

Joe has died because of his efforts to communicate feelings. Even though Carmela had originally compared the Americans to the Germans and the Fascists – "You're all alike, you, the Germans, the Fascists! All you people with guns! You're all the same!"[16] – Joe's senseless death angers her and galvanizes her resolve to fight the Germans. First, she hides Joe's body and his rifle. The Germans arrive, take over the fortress, and send Carmela for water, but she uncovers the rifle and shoots one of them. The camera then shifts back to the American squad on patrol. They hear Carmela's gunshot and hurry back to the fortress to discover Joe's dead body. Unaware that Carmela has attacked his killers, they mistakenly blame his death on the girl rather than on the Germans ("Why, that dirty little Eyetie!"[17]). As Carmela is cursed by Joe's comrades, the final shots of the episode focus first on three German soldiers; then there is a long shot of the Germans on a rock overlooking the ocean; the camera then pans downward to reveal Carmela's dead body sprawled on a rocky cliff, murdered by the Germans to avenge their comrade. Thus, the first attempt to cross cultural boundaries

Carmela attempting to hide Joe's body from the Germans. *Source*: Centro sperimentale di cinematografia Photograph Archives

results in the deaths of a representative of each culture and in complete misunderstanding by the Americans, who never appreciate Carmela's bravery and self-sacrifice.

Rossellini hardly allows his audience to draw its breath after the sudden deaths of Joe and Carmela, for the narrative voice-over moves quickly to the Naples sequence. Here we see the disastrous effects of the war upon the city through the perspective of a black American military policeman and a young boy named Pasquale, who "buys" Joe while he is drunk in order to steal everything he owns (both the purchase and the subsequent larceny being common occurrences in wartime Naples). The irony in this scene is a bitter one, for Rossellini shows an Italian buying an American black, a descendant of slaves who has paradoxically been sent to liberate the very Neapolitans who are now purchasing him. The distinction between reality and illusion is one of the first casualties of any war, and Rossellini emphasizes this very effectively when Joe and Pasquale witness a puppet show featuring the traditional Christian knights (white men) battling their usual enemies, the evil Moors (blacks). Such entertainment, popular in the south of Italy and based on figures taken from the Renaissance epic poetry of Ariosto and Tasso, is familiar to every Italian, but it must have seemed puzzling to Americans, who were accustomed to a different form of the Punch and Judy puppet tradition. Incensed by what he perceives to be a continuation of the racial oppression he has experienced at home, the black soldier leaps upon the stage, and in his inebriated condition, he tries to assist the Moorish puppet against his white opponent. Joe is ejected from the theater for his confusion of illusion and reality, and Rossellini employs this moment of cinematic self-reflexivity to remind us that the story he recounts is composed of equal elements of fact and fiction. The episode also contains the germ of Rossellini's future distrust in the unequivocal power of the cinematic image to convey moral truth, which he will explore in *La macchina ammazzacattivi*.

Away from the puppet theater, Joe dreams of a victorious return to America as a hero, complete with ticker-tape parades. But as he becomes sober, he realizes that as a black man in America, his lot is little better than the squalid conditions in which Pasquale is forced to live: "Goin' home! Goin' home? I don't want to go home! My house is an old shack with tin cans at the doors!"[18] Pasquale warns Joe, but in an Italian the American cannot understand, that he will steal his boots if Joe falls asleep, and his prophecy is soon fulfilled. Rossellini then immediately fades out to a moment three days later when Joe, on duty, picks up Pasquale for stealing Allied goods without realizing who the young thief really is. When he finally

In a drunken state, Joe confuses reality and illusion in the Neapolitan puppet show and defends the black Moorish knight against the white Christian knight.
Source: Centro sperimentale di cinematografia Photograph Archives

Joe takes Pasquale, the Neapolitan boy, back to Pasquale's squalid home inside a cave. *Source*: Centro sperimentale di cinematografia Photograph Archives

recognizes Pasquale as the boy who stole his boots, he forces Pasquale to return to his home to retrieve them. Joe discovers that Pasquale's home is actually a filthy cave teeming with hungry orphans and enormous families in the direst of straits and that his parents were killed in an Allied bombing raid. Astonished by such poverty and emotionally touched by the human suffering he has witnessed, Joe drops the boots and turns away. The subjective shots of the scene from Joe's point of view convey the empathy Joe feels for his fellow sufferers in a far more eloquent manner than any voice-over commentary could have done. Joe has taken the first step, that of understanding, toward becoming Pasquale's *paisà*.

The initial shots of the third sequence come from documentary footage showing German troops abandoning Rome and the arrival of the Allies. From this newsreel footage, Rossellini dissolves to a moment six months later when a prostitute named Francesca picks up a drunken American soldier named Fred who knows a bit of Italian (just as Francesca possesses a more than rudimentary knowledge of English). She takes him to a hotel, where in his drunken condition, Fred echoes the cynical opinion first voiced in the film by Carmela in the Sicilian sequence:

> Rome's full of girls like you! . . . Yeah! And now you're all alike! Before,
> it was different somehow. I remember when we first came into Rome
> – so long ago it was! You know, when we finally broke through. Girls

were all happy and laughing and fresh, full of color, beautiful . . . And now it's all different. You should've seen the one I knew – her name was Francesca.[19]

As Fred recalls a time when Roman women were more innocent and when the springtime of which Francesco spoke to Pina in *Roma città aperta* still seemed a real possibility, Rossellini dissolves to a flashback that shows how Fred and Francesca met earlier when Rome was liberated. Fred's tank stops outside Francesca's middle-class apartment building, and Fred gets out to ask for some water. During the flashback, which contains about eighteen shots that are taken from Fred's point of view, we learn that both Fred and Francesca have been studying Italian and English in an enthusiastic effort to communicate with each other's cultures. However, the economic deprivation following the city's liberation eventually forced Francesca onto the streets. Once again Rossellini moves by a dissolve back to the present in Francesca's bedroom. While Fred is sleeping, she leaves an address with the madam that will reveal to Fred when he awakens the location of the innocent

A drunken Fred speaks of the beautiful Italian girl he met when Rome was liberated without recognizing that the prostitute he has picked up is that same girl, Francesca. *Source*: Centro sperimentale di cinematografia Photograph Archives

75

Francesca, the beautiful girl dominating Fred's memory whom he met six months earlier. She experiences a renewal of hope and once again believes in the possibility of change and self-transformation. While she waits for him in the rain, Fred awakens sober, unaware that he has happiness within his grasp, and he tosses the address away, remarking to another soldier that it is only the address of a whore. Rossellini has set his problematic view of the end of innocence within a melodramatic plot based on the perennial male fantasy of the whore with a heart of gold, and the sequence exploits the codes of traditional fiction and filmmaking rather than those of film realism to achieve what must be considered, nevertheless, a deeply moving portrayal of the corruption and unhappiness that follows in the wake of war.

Of all the six sequences of *Paisà*, the Rome sequence is closest to traditional cinematic melodrama, an assessment strengthened by the episode's dramatic dissolves and its flashback technique, as well as by the fact that most of it was shot inside the same studio on Via degli Avignonesi in Rome where Rossellini had re-created the principal interiors of *Roma città aperta*. The sequence employs a traditional narrative device, a flashback, but it obeys an even more ancient literary convention associated with comedy. Two characters who know each other fail to recognize each other, thereby complicating the plot. Even the quality of the acting in this sequence improves, since no speaking roles of any importance are filled by nonprofessional actors.

It appears as if conventional filmmaking techniques took over the film here. The Roman sequence was the last of the six episodes to be shot, and there is at least the possibility that Rossellini was able to be more creative and innovative in his narrative techniques when he had his crew on location outside Rome and far away from his producers. Another plausible explanation for the marked difference between the style of this Roman sequence and that of the other five may be that according to the testimony of Rod Geiger, it was scripted primarily by Alfred Hayes, an American soldier hired by Rossellini as scriptwriter, with Sergio Amidei, who, in spite of his leftist opinions in politics, had thoroughly traditional notions about a well-constructed narrative plot. There is also universal agreement that Fellini made crucial contributions to all but this Roman episode. Although it has long been fashionable to overlook the importance of Fellini's written contributions to the birth of Italian neorealism, Fellini's absence from this sequence may well have had as important an impact as his contribution to the monastery episode in the fifth section of the film.[20]

The first three episodes of *Paisà* reveal failures of communication. With the Florentine episode, this atmosphere of hopelessness slowly begins to change. Whereas Fred spoke only broken Italian and his efforts to bridge the gap between his culture and that of Italy were rendered useless by his preconceived notions and the economic impact of the war upon Italian private life, the American nurse Harriet in the Florentine sequence has spent several years in Italy before the war and speaks Italian perfectly, and the heroic partisan leader named Lupo was apparently her lover. Hearing that he may be wounded, Harriet races away from her hospital duties on the south side of the city and crosses the Arno River with another partisan in search of him. After braving German bullets and witnessing the summary execution of Fascists by angry partisans, Harriet arrives only to learn that Lupo has died from his wounds. Her pain and commitment to assisting the Italian struggle are sharply contrasted to the aloofness demonstrated by two British officers who sit on a hill peering through binoculars at Giotto's tower in the center of town, both oblivious to the human suffering surrounding them.[21] Once again, an attempt to bridge the gap between two people from different cultures ends tragically, but an important shift in emphasis has subtly taken place. Rather than being a passive observer, the American protagonist of this episode takes on a more active role, and she may be said to represent a kind of empathetic progress.

The fifth episode, in the Apennine monastery, was drastically changed from Amidei's version to one scripted primarily by Fellini. In Amidei's earlier version, an American chaplain is forced to kill two Germans at Anzio in self-defense and reaches the monastery during a crisis of conscience. There his resolve hardens, he decides against desertion, and he returns to his vocation at the front. Such a figure would follow Amidei's ideological requirements for a positive hero struggling for a better world. However, at least one version of Amidei's episode, entitled "Il porco di Predappio" ("The Pig of Predappio") would have constituted a far more comic sequence.[22] It would have pictured a group of monks hoarding their animals from the Germans, including a prize pig, the proud property of a parish priest from Predappio, the birthplace of Benito Mussolini in Emilia-Romagna. The American chaplains of the final version of the sequence would arrive and offer the monks a terrible meal cooked from a collection of canned foods (a completely negative interpretation of American cooking that is totally reversed by Fellini's script, where the monks praise the quality of the American food in tins). As a means of demonstrating the superiority of Italian cooking (and, by implication, Italian civilization), the monks prepare a feast

British officers gaze at Giotto's tower, indifferent to the partisans dying in their struggle to liberate Florence. *Source*: Centro sperimentale di cinematografia Photograph Archives

fit for a Roman emperor in which the pièce de résistance is the parish priest's roasted pig. The episode was to end on the parish priest's remark to the chaplains that Italy could boast of two pigs from Predappio: the one the Americans knew most about (Mussolini) and the other, more praiseworthy pig served at their table!

Fellini's revision of Amidei's script may well have been suggested by Boccaccio's celebrated tale of Melchisedech and the three rings in *The Decameron*, a novella treating religious tolerance and the difficulty of attaining

Harriet braves sniper fire in the Florence sequence to reach her ex-lover, now a partisan leader, only to arrive too late. *Source*: Centro sperimentale di cinematografia Photograph Archives

In the monastery sequence, the three American chaplains are perplexed by the fasting of the Catholic monks, who are praying for the conversion of the two non-Catholic chaplains. *Source*: Centro sperimentale di cinematografia Photograph Archives

absolute truth. It also moves the story away from the comic ending suggested by Amidei's pig from Predappio toward a far more philosophical and enigmatic conclusion, a revision that may surprise viewers accustomed to considering Fellini to be essentially a comic filmmaker. While the war rages around them, three chaplains — a Catholic, a Protestant, and a Jew — visit a Franciscan monastery that seems untouched by the passing centuries or the present conflict. When the simple monks discover that Captain Martin, the Catholic, has never attempted to convert his two friends to the "true" faith, they decide to fast in order that God may provide the grace to lead these "two lost souls" to salvation, leaving the three Americans to eat by themselves as they pray together. When Captain Martin, who speaks Italian extremely well and obviously understands the culture of the country, realizes why the monks are fasting, he addresses them in an extraordinary manner that the film's viewers have always found puzzling: "I want to tell you that what you've given me is such a great gift that I feel I'll always be in your debt. I've found here that peace of mind I'd lost in the horrors and the trials of the war, a beautiful, moving lesson of humility, simplicity, and pure faith. Pax hominibus bonae voluntatis."[23]

Such a puzzling statement delivered in this emotionally charged context, where the Catholic monks could easily be suspected of bigotry and anti-Semitism, underlines the vast emotional distance separating the active chaplains from such simple, even simple-minded, friars. Martin's speech forces us to consider the possibility of irony. Are the monks providing a lesson in pure faith or one of religious intolerance? Many American viewers of this sequence will doubtless disagree with Captain Martin, who accepts the monks' fasting as an act of genuine, pure, simple religious faith. The key to the entire sequence must be found in the conception of Catholicism that both Fellini and Rossellini shared at this time (one that both of them would eventually abandon in their later careers). While rejecting the institutional trappings of the church, particularly its doctrinaire stands on certain social and moral issues, Fellini and Rossellini, like so many Italians, responded positively to the church's evangelical message of brotherhood and universal love. It would not be an exaggeration to state that the hotly contested movement away from social realism in the postwar Italian cinema toward what Rossellini once called the "cinema of Reconstruction" begins here in the enigmatic monastery episode scripted by Fellini with Rossellini's approval. It is significant that Fellini served as both scriptwriter and male lead for Rossellini's subsequent meditation on the meaning of Christian faith in the controversial episode of *L'amore* entitled *Il miracolo,* which created an international scandal only two years later. The journey on the so-called road beyond neorealism that Rossellini, Fellini, and Antonioni undertook in the 1950s was begun even as Rossellini and Fellini were in the process of completing with *Paisà* what must be considered Italian neorealism's most unusual and original work.

The final, Po Valley episode features an American liaison officer named Dale whose command of the Italian language reflects his almost complete integration into the partisan struggle. Here, more than in any other part of the film, Rossellini's highly mobile camera is brilliantly used to convey the circumscribed world of the partisans, as the frame never peers above the thin row of reeds in the marshy river basin, which provides the only cover from the Germans pursuing the partisans. The partisans are rounded up like animals by the Nazis, who observe the Geneva Conventions with the Allied advisers but execute the partisans the following dawn by pushing them into the river with their hands tied behind them and signs reading "Partisan" attached to the life jackets that keep the bodies afloat without saving the partisans from drowning. When Dale rushes forward to protest, he is shot down. The last image we see in the film is that of a floating partisan, while a voice-over remarks without emotion: "This happened in

Partisans bury one of their dead in a simple but moving ceremony in the Po River Valley. *Source*: Museum of Modern Art Film Stills Archives

the winter of 1944. At the beginning of spring, the war was over."[24]

The matter-of-fact manner in which the final episode is narrated has elicited a great deal of comment. Indeed, André Bazin's famous essay on Italian neorealism used it as the centerpiece of his analysis of Rossellini's style, which he defined as "elliptical." "A complex train of action is reduced to three or four brief fragments, in themselves already elliptical enough in comparison with the reality they are unfolding."[25] By employing six separate episodes with very different protagonists, Rossellini has already thwarted the primary thrust of conventional Hollywood narration – the audience's easy identification with a single hero throughout a whole film. His unrelenting and blunt presentation of the "facts" of the Italian campaign, whether portrayed in a purely documentary style or not, and his brisk movement from one story to another, without allowing the viewer the emotional climaxes and rest periods we have come to expect from Hollywood products, are in themselves revolutionary without considering *Paisà*'s equally original stylistic relationship to "reality."

Rossellini's film shows us episodes from the Allied liberation of Italy, but the facts it presents do not explain the film's greatness. The mutual encounter of two different cultures has been characterized by errors, failures of understanding, ambiguity, and ultimately by death and tragedy. Yet, the pessimism of the film is not Rossellini's final message, for the work provides a moving testimony to the human spirit. In the beginning of the film, Joe from Jersey dies on Sicilian soil almost by accident, unable to comprehend the people he came to liberate. At the conclusion of the film, Dale sacrifices his own life for his Italian comrades in a gesture that signifies the equality of all people fighting for liberty. He becomes a *paisà*, a kinsman to everyone struggling for a better world, a member of the same moral universe inhabited by both Don Pietro and Manfredi of *Roma città aperta*. Dale demonstrates that the value of a person's life is founded on love for fellow human beings, a Christian notion that transcends all the feeble intellectual attempts to comprehend or communicate by rational means alone. Ultimately, linguistic barriers and the problems of human communication, so brilliantly rendered by the various episodes in *Paisà*, fade away in the face of moral commitment.

5

La macchina ammazzacattivi
Doubts about the Movie Camera as a Morally Redemptive Force

The most creative phase of Italian neorealism took place within a single decade, from the early 1940s to the early 1950s. As we have already seen, a number of works produced during the fascist era are generally considered precursors to neorealist style, including the fictional documentaries by De Robertis, Genina's *L'assedio dell'Alcazar,* Rossellini's early war trilogy, as well as a few key dramatic films from the early 1940s unconnected with war themes, such as Visconti's *Ossessione (Obsession,* 1942), Blasetti's *Quattro passi fra le nuvole (A Stroll in the Clouds,* 1942), and De Sica's *I bambini ci guardano (The Children Are Watching Us,* 1942). There is universal agreement, however, that international recognition of bold neorealist innovation in cinematic art came only with the success of Rossellini's *Roma città aperta* and *Paisà.* On the other hand, critics have too often failed to realize that Rossellini and other important directors and scriptwriters identified with the advent of neorealism, such as Michelangelo Antonioni, Vittorio De Sica, Luchino Visconti, and Federico Fellini, began almost immediately after the early success of Rossellini's two films to move Italian cinema beyond a doctrinaire adherence to such critically praised elements of neorealist filmmaking as nonprofessional actors, documentary photography, authentic locations, and socially defined protagonists even as they were winning awards and critical praise at film festivals all over the world. Almost every truly original and innovative Italian director reacted negatively against an attempt on the part of some leftist or progressive critics to dictate what we would probably term today a "politically correct" cinema. Such critics wanted to prescribe a formula for Italian directors that would advance their political agenda, elevating various aspects of neorealist practice to the status of a rule to be followed. Naturally, the directors felt this was a threat to their creative independence. Once again, Rossellini was a pioneer, for as our examination of *Paisà* has demonstrated, the elements of an entirely different kind of cinema from that encouraged by the critical orthodoxy can be detected in the enigmatic monastery episode of *Paisà*.

Neorealist directors were always conscious of creating the *illusion* of reality in their works. As André Bazin so perceptively wrote in his seminal essay on Italian neorealism, "An Aesthetic of Realism: Neorealism (Cinematic Realism and the Italian School of the Liberation)," originally published in 1948, "realism in art can only be achieved in one way – through artifice."[1] In no sense did these consummate artists merely photograph the "reality" that existed around them. As Roy Armes has noted, this consciousness of their medium as an artistic artifact also implied the retention of the entire apparatus of commercial filmmaking, and since the construction of an artistic product presupposed artistic choices, the paradoxical result of neorealism was to strengthen the role of the director as auteur.[2] Thus, it was no accident that the critics of the French journal *Cahiers du Cinéma,* many of whom were themselves to become directors and to adopt the famous *politique des auteurs,* as they called it, embraced Rossellini's neorealism precisely because his example championed the director's artistic control of his product, as opposed to control by producer or studio.[3]

A number of the formulae for neorealist style favored by many critics also had aesthetic implications that explain, in large measure, why the most original of the Italian directors would almost immediately attempt to transcend them. We have already seen how Rossellini mixed nonprofessional actors with professionals in his major neorealist films. Rejecting professional actors meant rejecting the portrayal of complex psychological problems in the cinema and concentrating on social or economic issues, and when this subject matter no longer satisfied the neorealists, the professional actor quickly replaced the nonprofessional. The neorealist preference for authentic locations rather than shooting in studios has been overemphasized, but it is, as Armes notes, even more crucial to the neorealist style than nonprofessional actors, for on-location shooting practically demands a particular kind of photography that privileges the newsreel quality of the image and eschews what Armes calls "chiaroscuro effects or expressionistic devices."[4] Films shot in this manner would ultimately have less to say about intricate psychological states of mind than about conditions in society.

While overzealous progressive critics sought to place neorealist directors within an aesthetic straitjacket, the best of these artists immediately grasped the aesthetic impasse into which a complete adherence to such neorealist formulae would take the Italian cinema. If there was very little agreement among these artists during the neorealist decade about what Italian neorealism was or should be, there was almost universal consensus about the negative impact that would result from forcing Italian cinema into a single politically correct path – that of social or socialist realism.[5] Federico Fellini, for example, remarked that concentrating upon economic and social problems, as the greatest of the neorealist films certainly did, was not sufficient in the post-Reconstruction era:

> Remember, after the war our themes were ready-made. Primitive problems: how to survive, war, peace. These problems were topical, immediate, brutal. But today the problems are different. Surely the neorealists would not hope for the continuation of war and poverty just because it gave them good material. I think the editors of *Cinema nuovo* are partly responsible for what you call our uncertainty. Instead of realizing that neorealism was a beginning, they assumed it was an end, a golden age. Some of the neorealists seem to think that they cannot make a film unless they have a man in old clothes in front of the camera. That is not right. We have not even scratched the surface of Italian life.[6]

In another often-quoted interview with Fellini on the so-called crisis of neorealism, Fellini defined neorealism not by its content but by its style and moral perspective: "Why should people go to the movies, if films show reality only through a very cold, objective eye? It would be much better just to walk around in the street. For me, neorealism means looking at reality with an honest eye – but any kind of reality: not just social reality, but also spiritual reality, metaphysical reality, anything man has inside him."[7]

Another major figure of the neorealist era, Michelangelo Antonioni, who had been one of the most influential critics associated with the journal *Cinema* in the late fascist period, a journal that had advocated moving Italian cinema toward social realism even before Italian neorealism was born, also called for a different kind of cinema that was more sensitive to problems other than the obvious socioeconomic ones that emerged in the immediate postwar years:

> The neorealism of the postwar period, when reality itself was so searing and immediate, attracted attention to the relationship existing between

the character and surrounding reality. It was precisely this relationship which was important and which created an appropriate cinema. Now, however, when for better or worse reality has been normalized once again, it seems to me more interesting to examine what remains in the characters from their past experiences. This is why it no longer seems to me important to make a film about a man who has had his bicycle stolen. That is to say, about a man whose importance resides (primarily and exclusively) in the fact that he has his bicycle stolen. . . . Now that we have eliminated the problem of the bicycle (I am speaking metaphorically), it is important to see what there is in the mind and in the heart of this man who has had his bicycle stolen, how he has adapted himself, what remains in him of his past experiences, of the war, of the period after the war, of everything that has happened to him in our country.[8]

Antonioni's remarks about a stolen bicycle refer to one of the most popular of all neorealist works, Vittorio De Sica's *Ladri di biciclette* (*The Bicycle Thief*, 1948), which appeared during the very year Rossellini began work on *La macchina ammazzacattivi*. But like Rossellini, De Sica, whose neorealist classics seem so closely tied to current events in the immediate postwar period, felt a need to move away from an emphasis on socioeconomic problems toward a self-conscious treatment of the interplay between illusion and reality, fact and fiction. This, in fact, is what De Sica did in his marvelous comic fable about the rich and the poor, *Miracolo a Milano* (*Miracle in Milan*, 1950), which De Sica said he made in order to resolve problems of "form and style," and not in order to resolve political or philosophical questions that a serious examination of poverty in postwar Milan would require.[9] Rossellini's statements about the cinema during this period echo this same dissatisfaction with neorealism as a cinema of purely socioeconomic problems.

Shooting on *La macchina ammazzacattivi* began in June 1948, and according to one recent critical analysis of Rossellini's films, Rossellini spent only three months filming on location, working only thirty days during those three months.[10] Moreover, Rossellini often left the set in his automobile for Rome and did not return until midnight, thereby forcing the troupe to wait for his assistant directors to shoot the day's scenes. Ultimately, the completion of the film was delayed for a number of reasons, and the final editing was accomplished by Rossellini's assistants under the direction of the producer. However, the director's cavalier attitude toward his creation

86

must not be construed as lack of interest in it. It is more likely that the turbulent personal problems in his life – the ending of his affair with Anna Magnani and the beginning of an even more momentous affair with Ingrid Bergman – are more than a little responsible for the delay in the film's release until 1952, three years after work was completed on the set. In fact, in an interview with Fernaldo Di Giammatteo given in 1948 when Rossellini was engaged in editing the material he had shot to that date, Rossellini somewhat surprisingly described *La macchina ammazzacattivi* as his "most original film" in a general discussion of the future of Italian neorealism:

> The type of realism that I inaugurated with *Roma città aperta* and *Paisà* is no longer of any use today. It was fine then when it seemed a crime not to suggest to men the necessity of becoming conscious of the world in which we lived and of the need to sink our hands into this world to feel what it was made of. Today other things concern me. Today I think one must discover a new and solid base for constructing and for representing man as he is, in the marriage that exists in him between poetry and reality, desire and action, dream and life. For this reason I made *L'amore* and *La macchina ammazzacattivi*, which is perhaps my most original film. Its framework is modest, its tone is more facile, but sometimes one must descend if one wishes to say things that everybody can understand. On the other hand, it is precisely in *La macchina ammazzacattivi* that my new convictions are summed up and explained, and simplicity is no bother in such a case.[11]

By 1952, when the film was released, as an often-cited interview with Mario Verdone given in that year demonstrates, Rossellini had not fundamentally changed his mind about the importance of *La macchina ammazzacattivi*. In this interview, Rossellini defines realism quite simply as "the artistic form of the truth," emphasizing that realism was a moral position, not an aesthetic one requiring a fixed cinematic style or only a certain kind of thematic content.[12] Rossellini would maintain this position during his entire life and it would be reiterated forcefully during his beginnings as a director in the new medium of television. In the Verdone interview, Rossellini listed four constant elements in all his films: *coralità*, or a choral quality; a documentary manner of observing and analyzing; religiosity; and fantasy, which is the opposite of the documentary technique and which must be balanced with it so that one aspect of his style does not suffocate the other. As Rossellini notes in the interview, *La macchina ammazzacattivi* was a film reflecting both his search for a new style and a personal artistic crisis that the film was intended to resolve; in it, Rossellini tried to draw nearer to the commedia dell'arte. It was precisely the force of fantasy that Rossellini tried to present in this puzzling film, a quality Rossellini claimed to find in abundance on the Amalfi coast, where it was filmed and where he had already shot several episodes of *Paisà* and *Il miracolo*:

> *La macchina ammazzacattivi* contains my wanderings on the Amalfi coast: the places where we were happy and where we were in love; where there are poor devils who are convinced that they have seen a demon; where one told me one day: "Yes, I saw him, the werewolf. Yesterday evening, I ran over him on my bicycle." They are crazy, people inebriated with the sun. But they know how to live by employing a power that few of us possess: the power of the imagination.[13]

These ideas were even more forcefully presented in perhaps Rossellini's most influential interview, that given in 1954 to Eric Rohmer (writing under the pseudonym Maurice Schérer) and François Truffaut for *Cahiers du Cinéma*. When asked about the shift in his cinematic style from the early neorealist classics, which some critics believed had taken place after *Stromboli*, Rossellini's reply seems to echo the previously cited statements of dissatisfaction with continuing a cinema emphasizing the problems of the war and the immediate postwar period:

> In my opinion – not that I set that much store by it – there is no break at all. I think I am the same human being looking at things in the same way. But one is moved to take up other themes, interest is shifted somewhere else, you have to take other paths; you cannot go on shooting in ruined cities forever. Too often we make the mistake of letting ourselves be hypnotized by a particular milieu, by the feel of a particular time. But life has changed, the war is over, the cities have been rebuilt. It was the story of the reconstruction that had to be told.[14]

La macchina ammazzacattivi thus occupies an important place in Rossellini's cinema, even though it was not a success at the box office and experienced an unfortunate production history that caused it to be released three years after it was shot. Its value lies in the fact that it helps to explain the transition from Rossellini's war trilogy to a very different kind of cinema altogether that would find its fullest artistic expression in *Viaggio in Italia,* the best of the films made during the so-called Bergman era. The plot is extremely complicated, as we should expect from a film linked by the director himself to the traditional commedia dell'arte and scripted in part by the playwright Eduardo De Filippo, who was certainly the greatest contemporary writer in the Neapolitan regional tradition. The film opens with the visit to a small town on the Amalfi coast by a former American soldier (played by Bill Tubbs, the chaplain of *Paisà*) who has brought his wife (played by Helen Tubbs) and his niece (played by Marilyn Buferd, Miss America of 1946) to see where he landed a few years ago to liberate the town where today he hopes to build a resort hotel on the spot where the villagers bury their dead. While driving along the winding coastal road toward the town with one of the townspeople the soldier met during the war, they think they have struck an old man with the car (who miraculously appears on the road within a frame that opens in a partial wipe), but the man is nowhere to be found. After learning that the town's patron saint is Saint Andrew (with the implication that the old man might well be he), the storyline shifts abruptly to Celestino Esposito, the town's photographer, who has been asked to take photographs of the religious procession on the festival day of Saint Andrew as the populace goes to the shore to bless the fishing boats. The same old man that the American believes he struck with his car can be seen several times in the crowd, captured by a zoom shot to emphasize his identity. Later that evening, the old man turns up at Celestino's shop to ask for a place to sleep, and when the photographer complains that Saint Andrew seems to have forgotten the town, the old man tells Celestino that good men must act and destroy evil people. Having witnessed an argument between the town policeman and Celestino that afternoon, he instructs Celestino to fetch a photograph of the policeman and then tells him to take a photograph of the photograph. Celestino discovers from the screams in the apartment above his shop that the policeman has been frozen in the exact position he held in the photograph. Celestino now has the means to combat evil, even though the old man has magically disappeared, and it seems obvious to him that the old man was Saint Andrew in disguise.

Armed with this apparently lethal camera (the *màcchina* of the film's title; the word for "machine" also means "camera" in Italian), Celestino attempts to right a number of wrongs in his town, all of which are caused by greed and arise because of the sudden good fortune that seems to have arrived in town with the appearance of the old man, supposedly the town's patron saint. The government in Rome suddenly announces a disbursement of eleven million lire for the town, and this windfall ignites the cupidity of everyone but Celestino: Signor Cuccurullo (the owner of the town's truck fleet, which carries the fish to market) wants a tunnel built to facilitate his commerce; Signor Del Bello (the owner of most of the fishing boats) wants a dam built to protect his fleet; the mayor supports the construction of the

Celestino receives magic powers for his camera from his strange visitor.
Source: Museum of Modern Art Film Stills Archives

American hotel (he hopes to profit from it, since he is the ex-soldier's friend); and even the priest shows his selfishness, advocating that the scarce funds from Rome be spent on refurbishing the false baroque facade of the town's church, replacing it with an equally false Byzantine style complete with fake Byzantine mosaics! As the town council argues, the town's rich but avaricious loan shark, Donna Amalia, walks into the meeting and threatens the council with calling in all their various debts to her if they do not use the windfall money to erect a monument to her dead husband, who was a self-proclaimed poet. Celestino is not completely immune to the disease of selfishness, since he thinks the town needs a new sewer because of the odor permeating his shop. When Donna Amalia orders Celestino (who, like the town council, owes Donna Amalia rent money he has not paid since 1934) to make an enlargement of a photograph of her husband, Celestino does this by covering up Donna Amalia in the photograph and taking a new picture of her husband. But the paper he uses to block out the wife has several pinprick-sized holes in it, and forgetting his new powers, Celestino thus freezes Donna Amalia without meaning to do so.

The plot now really begins to become complicated. Upon Donna Amalia's paralysis by Celestino's camera, the major debtors, Del Bello and Cuccurullo, who, like most citizens in the small town, are the woman's relatives,

Donna Amalia, the town's richest woman, in bed surrounded by her entourage and frozen by Celestino's magic camera. *Source*: Museum of Modern Art Film Stills Archives

seize her will and are horrified to discover that she has performed an act of Christian charity, bequeathing all her wealth to the three poorest citizens of the village. Celestino observes them hiding the will and is beaten for his trouble when he demands that it be given back to the authorities. His indignation over their actions and his remorse for having frozen such a "generous" woman drive him to begin the punishment of evil that was requested by the old man who granted the photographer his magic powers. Here a number of comic subplots become operative, for the American family has been lodged with the people that Celestino will attack first with his camera. As he freezes one citizen after another, the Americans are forced to move from house to house, never quite understanding why they have to do so. A second subplot involves a lighthearted parody of Shakespeare by picturing the love affair between Giulietta, the daughter of Del Bello, and Romeo, the son of Cuccurullo. While their fathers quarrel and fight, Celestino helps the two meet through the back window of his photography shop.

As Celestino freezes one after another of his fellow citizens, he becomes more and more self-righteous and indignant over the evil and selfishness in the world around him. When he learns that the three poorest of the town's

The Americans visiting Celestino's village find the immobilized body of yet another of Celestino's victims, forcing them to change houses one more time. *Source*: Museum of Modern Art Film Stills Archives

Celestino attends the funeral of one of the town's citizens whom he has eliminated with his magic camera. *Source*: Museum of Modern Art Film Stills Archives

citizens, who are to receive Donna Amalia's fortune, are actually thieves, he freezes them and then decides to eliminate the whole town by making a group photograph of the entire population. His friend the town doctor tries to stop him, but Celestino strikes the doctor and thinks he has killed him. Filled with remorse, he decides that he will eliminate himself instead, but first he wants to do away with the old man who started all the mischief in the first place. When Celestino tries his powers on the old man, however, he transmogrifies in a magic puff of smoke, revealing himself to be a minor devil rather than a saint. When Celestino instructs the devil to make the sign of the cross, all the individuals Celestino has frozen come back to life, and everything returns to normal.

This schematic outline of the film's plot places it squarely within the commedia dell'arte tradition that Rossellini mentioned in his interview, a theatrical tradition that Eduardo De Filippo as both playwright and actor in the regional-dialect theater of Naples did so much to perpetuate in the twentieth century. But commedia dell'arte refers specifically to a *professional* troupe of actors, not the nonprofessionals preferred by some neorealist critics. The term *arte* in the name refers not to "art" but to a guild or association of professional actors. True to his usual formula, Rossellini mixes professional actors, such as William Tubbs, with nonprofessionals in *La macchina ammazzacattivi*. The most important role played by a nonprofessional is that of the photographer, performed by Gennaro Pisano, a carpenter. The significant links between Rossellini's film and the commedia dell'arte tradition lie elsewhere: in the film's reliance on vivid comic action, visual effects, humor, and a conception of film character based on the comic masks typical of this theatrical tradition.

Celestino's visitor is finally revealed to be a demon with horns. *Source*: Museum of Modern Art Film Stills Archives

Rossellini informs the spectator that the conventions of the commedia dell'arte are operative by beginning the film with a prologue in verse that precedes the arrival of the Americans and their drive toward the village:

> Here's our comedy, my friends,
> and here's the prologue.
> What do we need? A clear day
> and a calm sea. Now, a cardboard
> mountain . . . deserted it's sad
> until we cover it with houses.
> And here's city hall with its fountain.
> And here are the grand houses of the rich.
> And now that we've set the scene,
> here are the characters.
> All thieves, schemers, conceited swindlers,
> lazy, malicious and silly.
> Servile or insolent, complaining and never content . . .
> In the end, nice or not,
> they resemble each other a lot.
> Now let the comedy start.
> Listen and laugh with all your heart.[15]

True to the best traditions of the commedia dell'arte, Rossellini's characters all share the same comic mask and are dominated by selfishness, greed, and self-interest. And in what must certainly be a comic swipe at orthodox neorealist critics, the poor are in this depiction as despicable as the wealthy. Their membership in the proletariat grants them no special dispensation.[16] As a result, although such one-dimensional figures are very different from the more psychologically complex figures of Rossellini's Bergman period, they at least abandon any pretense of being determined by their social surroundings, as the protagonists of neorealist films usually were.

Even more important to the polemical intent of the film are the visuals that accompany the introductory verse prologue. While the words tell us that all the characters in the comedy are alike, they also emphasize the completely fictitious, artificial, and consciously created nature of what will follow. As the voice-over delivers the prologue, a large hand and arm in extremely mannered, theatrical movements arrange paper cutouts of all the elements of the story: the mountain, then the houses, then city hall with its fountain, and finally the characters, both rich and poor. These theatrical flourishes serve to foreground the contrived nature of what is to follow, and the hand presents each individual cutout by means of continuous dissolves, a means of transition in the cinema that dramatically calls attention to itself. The prologue thus transforms what might have been only a simple comedy into a consciously self-reflexive film that makes a statement about the art of the cinema.

Immediately after the prologue, Rossellini dissolves from his stage set to the first scene of his narrative, a view of the Americans' car speeding down a hill. The hand of the unspecified creator of the scene (a puppet master or a theatrical *capocomico*, who serves as the theatrical equivalent of a movie director) lingers on the screen for a few seconds, superimposed to effect the transition from artifice to "reality." After the apparent accident in which the car seems to strike the old man, the American's niece sees the inscription "Viva Saint Andrew!" on a rock by the road and asks who he is. At that point, Rossellini effects a partial wipe that moves from the middle of the frame to its sides, suggesting the opening of a theater curtain. With the closing of this curtain wipe, the Americans and the spectators believe they have learned that the old man is actually Saint Andrew, a belief that the conclusion of the film shows to be incorrect. But because Rossellini reveals this false identification of the old man and Saint Andrew by means of such a dramatic cinematic editing technique, he is simultaneously also questioning the ultimate ability of the cinema to communicate true information.[17]

Rossellini is concerned with the symbolic importance of the camera and, by extension, the nature of photography itself. Celestino seems to represent a comical caricature of neorealist mythology about the magic powers of the movie camera. He believes the camera can serve as a means of separating reality from illusion, good from evil, substance from appearance. Photography for Celestino (and for many of the more doctrinaire neorealist theorists) is a metaphor for a way of knowing, for a means of apprehending essential moral and ethical facts. It enables Celestino, so he believes, to penetrate the surface of events to the bedrock of reality and to fulfill a godlike role in his small village, not unlike that a film director plays on a set, where he or she, too, is all powerful. It is thus very significant that Celestino does not perform his miraculous photographic feats by directly duplicating objects from the "real" world on his film stock. Instead, the power given to him by the old man only operates when he films an object self-reflexively by taking a photograph of another photograph, not the object itself. As any good Platonist knows, Celestino thus remains not one step but two steps removed from the world of tangible phenomena and is engaged in the essentially self-reflexive act of producing a work of art from another work of art, not directly producing art from reality.

While presenting us with an elaborate comic portrait of Celestino's self-delusory activity, Rossellini is also emphasizing a fundamental trait of the cinema. Photography and, by extension, the cinema as a branch of this art form of mechanical reproduction are incapable of separating good from evil or readily distinguishing reality from appearance. When objects are photographed, the act of photography does not in itself have any interpretative or cognitive value whatsoever. It is the perspective of the photographer that gives the act of photographic reproduction meaning, not the technical operation involved. As Rossellini and other neorealist directors often argued, neorealism was first a moral position before it was an aesthetic or technical point of view. To photograph or film from a particular perspective, the photographer or director must start from a moral or ethical position that lends itself to creating a work of art. In Rossellini's *La macchina ammaz-zacattivi*, Celestino has no truly superior moral position on which to stand, no fixed point that grants him authentic moral superiority over his fellow townspeople. Ultimately, he discovers that he and they are all motivated by self-interest and he is no better than they are, except that his own egotism takes the form of a seemingly benevolent desire to punish the wicked. And Celestino gets everything wrong. He takes what is revealed to be a demon to be the town's patron saint, apparently kills his friend the town doctor in a moment of madness, and generally makes a complex muddle of all his good intentions.

Celestino's comic misadventures are presented within the framework of a caricature, a grossly exaggerated collection of individuals who would rarely be encountered in society. But the commedia dell'arte conventions require characters defined as stock types – in this case, all dominated by a single selfish emotion. Rossellini ends the film with a rhymed epilogue suggesting a moral that, along with the opening prologue, provides a frame for the actions of his characters. The very fact that the storyline develops within such a frame is yet another device for foregrounding the metacinematic aspects of the film, just as literary classics with even more complex framing devices (such as *The Decameron* and *The Arabian Nights*) are ultimately about storytelling itself. And the moral of the epilogue is a message that orthodox neorealists would certainly find objectionable:

> We'll take down the sets, my friends.
> The play is over. Here's the moral:
> Do good but don't overdo it!
> Avoid evil, for your own sake.
> Don't be too hasty in judging others.
> Think twice before you punish anyone.

> I'll leave now for time does fly,
> So I'll take my bow and say goodbye.

Not only has Rossellini defined the camera as a morally neutral instrument, completely dependent upon an act of interpretation that precedes the moment of artistic creation (in this case, photography), but he has shown the camera to be not a means of acquiring knowledge of social reality but, instead, a fallible instrument that reflects not reality but human subjectivity and error. *La macchina ammazzacattivi* questions the cognitive potential of the camera and undermines the belief that good and evil are easily distinguished. Moreover, the sense of moral indignation over the exploitation of the poor by the rich, so central an element in all of the greatest neorealist films, seems now to have been abandoned.

It would be a mistake to equate the artistic merits of *La macchina ammazzacattivi* to those of Rossellini's greatest works. But it would also be critically incorrect to ignore the film, as so many critics of Rossellini have done in the past. A flawed, imperfect work, it nevertheless serves as testimony to the transition taking place in Rossellini's career from neorealism to an entirely different kind of cinema that would find its most felicitous expression in his work with Ingrid Bergman.

6
Viaggio in Italia
Ingrid Bergman and a New Cinema
of Psychological Introspection

The history of the Italian critical reception of *Viaggio in Italia* reflects a singular chronicle of incomprehension, whereas in France the film was greeted with exaggerated, sometimes delirious praise. Attacks upon the film in Italy surpassed previous levels of invective. For example, one article advised Rossellini to find another means of employment:

> The only possibility still remaining to Rossellini in considering himself a great director is that of definitively retiring from the screen and of removing from circulation his last four or five films. To change one's profession in certain circumstances is, without a doubt, the wisest thing one can do.[1]

Another venomous review found fault with every detail of the film:

> *Viaggio in Italia* does nothing but confirm the absolute, progressive, and irremediable decadence of Rossellini. It is sad to have to say of a director who has given us notable, even if overrated, films such as *Roma città aperta* and *Paisà* what we have to say. But it is also incomprehensible how an artist can reach similar disequilibria in his work, stooping to such infamies as *Viaggio in Italia*. In this film, there is no subject, no dialogue, no script, no direction. It is a jumble of images that revolve around emptily, tediously, without the slightest glimmer of interest.... *Viaggio in Italia* is more than an ugly film. It is a true and proper insult to the intelligence of the audience.[2]

By 1953, the critical establishment in Italy had turned against Rossellini for a variety of reasons. Conservative critics and some Catholic writers were incensed by Rossellini's private life and his scandalous liaison with Ingrid Bergman, although in France, Catholic critics were not puritanical conservatives and championed his films. Leftist and progressive critics did not jump to Rossellini's defense, as they might have done for other artists, because they were disturbed by Rossellini's turn away from strictly socio-economic themes with an overtly ideological slant. Thus, critics on both the Left and the Right reacted negatively to the most original aesthetic contributions of Rossellini's new introspective cinema.

The glowing tributes to Rossellini in France were also motivated by something more than intelligent recognition of the innovations of these films. Most critics tend to praise the kinds of films they themselves like or would make if they could, and the tributes to Rossellini by writers associated with what would eventually become the French New Wave and with the journal *Cahiers du Cinéma* were often the reflection of other polemical issues these intellectuals were debating at the time. In 1958, in one of the periodical votes on the all-time best films, which French critics love so much, Rossellini's *Viaggio in Italia* was ranked third behind Murnau's *Sunrise* and Renoir's *The Rules of the Game* but ahead of Eisenstein, Griffith, Welles, Dreyer, Mizoguchi, Vigo, von Stroheim, Hitchcock, and Chaplin by voters that included André Bazin, Jean-Luc Godard, François Truffaut, Claude Chabrol, Jacques Rivette, and Erich Rohmer.[3] In Rivette's assessment of the film for *Cahiers du Cinéma*, he made the most famous of all such comments on the film, remarking that "if there is a modern cinema, this is it," and that "with the appearance of *Viaggio in Italia,* all films have suddenly aged ten years."[4] Erich Rohmer declared that the public's negative reaction to the film paralleled the reaction of an ignorant public to impressionist art or the modernist music of Stravinsky: "As deliberately as Manet's refusal of *chiaroscuro,* the author of *Viaggio in Italia* scorns the easy choice – of a cinematic language underlaid with fifty years of use. Before Rossellini even the most inspired and original of film-makers would feel duty-bound to use the legacy of his precursors."[5] In a letter to Guido Aristarco, the editor of the Marxist journal *Cinema Nuovo,* André Bazin defended Rossellini's new direction after his neorealist trilogy, making another comparison between film and art:

> Neorealism discovers in Rossellini the style and the resources of abstraction. To have a regard for reality does not mean that what one does in fact is to pile up appearances. On the contrary, it means that one strips the appearances of all that is not essential, in order to get at the totality in its simplicity. The art of Rossellini is linear and melodic. True, several of his films make one think of a sketch: more

is implicitly in the line than it actually depicts. But is one to attribute such sureness of line to poverty of invention or to laziness? One would have to say the same of Matisse.[6]

These French writers and the critics and directors influenced by them have always reserved a special place for *Viaggio in Italia* in their admiration. Godard's *Le mépris* (*Contempt,* 1963) may be based on a novel by Alberto Moravia, but it is aesthetically indebted to Rossellini. Bernardo Bertolucci's background in film was largely gained from time spent in Paris absorbing the ideas of the group associated with *Cahiers,* and in his first important film, *Prima della rivoluzione* (*Before the Revolution,* 1964), one of his characters, a *cinéphile* who has seen *Viaggio in Italia* fifteen times, declares, "Remember, you cannot live without Rossellini."

Certainly, it was not the plot or thematic content of *Viaggio in Italia* that marked a revolution in filmmaking. The film follows a trip to Naples by an English couple, Alexander and Katherine Joyce – played by a thoroughly unlikable George Sanders and Ingrid Bergman – who have come to sell a villa their Uncle Homer has left them. While in Italy, the couple, either separately or together, visit the usual tourist sites – Capri, the Naples archeological museum, the lava fields of Vesuvius, Pompeii, the catacombs of Fontanelle – and their marriage begins to disintegrate. A short time after they have decided to seek a divorce, they have a change of heart during a

A typical shot of Alexander with his back turned away from Katherine, underlining their lack of communication. *Source*: Museum of Modern Art Film Stills Archives

religious procession in a small town on the Amalfi coast and embrace, seemingly willing to give their marriage another chance. Rossellini himself has underlined the conventional nature of a plot that juxtaposes Anglo-Saxon rigidity and inability to experience or express deep emotions with Mediterranean spontaneity and emotional depth:

> Civilization can be divided, figuratively speaking, into two categories: "toga" civilization, the civilization of men who still (morally speaking, of course) dress in robes; and "sewing" civilization, the civilization of men who have had to cover their bodies with the sewn hides of beasts in order to survive. The result is two quite different kinds of men. "Sewing" man is, logically enough, a highly efficient individual, while "toga" man has an easier, more relaxed view of life. What I tried to do, then, was to bring two specimens of "sewing" man into a completely "toga" world – a world which has after all made such a great contribution to the creation of modern civilization. And then I simply observed them – that's how *Viaggio in Italia* began.[7]

It would serve little purpose to analyze the collection of clichés Rossellini's "theory" (if it can be called such) contains. Film directors are not supposed to be metaphysicians, and Rossellini's ex cathedra pronouncements quite often reflect a naiveté that is surprising. To employ the contemporary vernacular, Rossellini brought a rigidly "uptight" English couple to sensual, fun-loving Naples to loosen them up a bit, and the impact of their visit managed to change their lives (presumably for the better).

Films and literary works reflecting a similar theme are numerous. It is not Rossellini's story but the way in which it was told that struck so many sensitive critics as highly original. The many references in the previously cited French critics' assessments of the film should be remembered here, for all of them, with their comparisons to Manet, Matisse, or Stravinsky, emphasized the work's *modernism* and its refusal to incorporate traditional film language into its narrative. José Guarner sums up Rossellini's surprisingly original treatment of what must be judged a banal plot by pointing out that although the plot concerns the breakup of a marriage, the film is not a tragedy; although it ends in reconciliation, it is not a comedy; and although it focuses on Italy, it is not a documentary; in fact, it fits none of the traditional Hollywood generic classifications, since "as a film about reality and time, it comes into the sphere of the essay."[8]

Perhaps in no other Rossellini film is the director's refusal to follow conventional Hollywood expectations of spectacle more marked than in

Viaggio in Italia, and this single fact alone certainly explains the commercial failure of the film as well as many of the critical attacks from conservative critics and hosannas from the avant-garde. First and foremost, Rossellini ignored the traditional reliance upon a literary script. Although Vitaliano Brancati, one of Italy's better novelists, was his scriptwriter, Rossellini, as was his habit, did not give a complete shooting script to his actors. In response to a question about his reputation for shooting without a script and improvisation on the set, Rossellini declared that this was "partly a myth," since he carried the continuity of his films in his head, and his pockets were always full of notes:

> Still, I must admit I have never really understood the need to have a shooting script unless it's to reassure the producers. What could be more absurd than the left-hand column: *medium shot [plan américain] – lateral travelling shot – pan and frame . . .* ? It's a bit like a novelist breaking down his book into sentences: on page 212, an imperfect subjunctive, then a complement to an indirect object . . . etc.! As for the right-hand column, that is the dialogue: I don't improvise it sys-tematically; it's written a long time in advance, and if I don't reveal it until the last moment it's because I don't want the actor, or the actress, to be too familiar with it. I also manage to keep that control of the actor by rehearsing very little and shooting fast, without too many takes. . . . In short, I don't work any differently from my col-leagues; I just dispense with the hypocrisy of the shooting script.[9]

Nevertheless, Rossellini's habitual practice on the set must have been substantially different from traditional Hollywood practice, for in George Sanders's memoirs, Rossellini is mercilessly attacked for being "deficient in what I might call the serious approach to movie-making" not only because there was no script but also because efficient organization was lacking.[10] His reaction to Rossellini's methods was so negative that he tried unsuc-cessfully to beg off working on the film, only to discover that Rossellini's financial backing depended on his presence in the movie.

Sanders's recollection of his work with Rossellini is valuable, for his views reflect a completely conventional attitude toward filmmaking. Nowhere does he completely misunderstand Rossellini's aesthetic in *Viaggio in Italia* more thoroughly than in his description of one of the most important sequences in the film: Katherine's visit to the National Archeological Museum in Naples, which occurs as soon as the couple arrive in Naples. Sanders, most audiences, and not a few traditional critics reacted in the same fashion to this scene. For Sanders, the scene consisted of a series of shots of Bergman admiring the statuary, nodding in appreciation as an old guide explained the various works:

> While it did not seem to me that these scenes were making the most of Miss Bergman's very considerable talents as an actress, they were quite interesting to watch for the first few hours or so. By the end of two weeks, however, my interest was reduced to a state bordering on stupefaction. Nevertheless, it was impossible to say what contribution these scenes made to the picture as a whole, as the story of the film was never understood at any time, by anyone, least of all the audience when the picture was released.[11]

Sanders's indictment covers a number of "deficiencies" he saw in Rossellini's work, the same weaknesses avant-garde critics have praised as its strengths. For Sanders, the scene was boring because it did not exploit the emotional potential of a Hollywood star and did not seem to fit into the larger, dramatic construction that a traditional dramatic script would usually embody. As a result, the audience predictably rejected the film. Ingrid Bergman's autobiography reveals that she had the same misgivings about this scene.[12]

Yet, if we examine the sequence in the completed film, we see exactly how wrong both Ingrid Bergman and George Sanders were. In fact, the scene is anything but boring and represents a perfect introduction to Rossellini's theme of the conflict of two different civilizations. As Jacques Rivette perceptively noted, "nothing in Rossellini better betokens the great filmmaker than those vast chords formed within his films by all the shots of eyes *looking*."[13] Each of the five visits Katherine makes in the film to various tourist sites – the National Archeological Museum, the site of the Cumean Sibyl, the lava fields near Vesuvius, the Fontanelle catacombs, and the excavations at Pompeii – all emphasize the theme of looking, but Rossellini avoids the usual banalities associated with tourism at these locations and employs each scene to reveal something profound about Katherine and her relationship with her husband. In the museum, for example, Rossellini's extremely mobile camera tracks, pans, and cranes about in the museum, always beginning a shot with the work of art in question (usually classical nudes) but ending the shot, without a cut in the editing, on the expression of Katherine. As a result, we are presented within a single, complex take not only the traditional, objective documentary of conventional art films but a much more interesting subjective point of view as well. As often as possible, Rossellini avoids the traditional Hollywood shot/reaction shot, where the audience first observes a character, then immediately looks at what the character sees, and finally observes the character's reaction to what he or she sees. By employing a single long take, Rossellini forces the spectator into an active, rather than a passive, role because the audience must search in the photographic image of the artwork for clues to the character's reaction. Meaning is created out of the way characters react to what they see.[14] Moreover, the museum guide's comments help to emphasize the contrast between the classical civilization's acceptance of the nude body and Katherine's puritanical sexual repression. For instance, the guide remarks that a particular nude torso of Venus is more beautiful than another one because it represents a more mature body, but when he asks Katherine if she agrees, her curt reply ("I wouldn't know") and her abrupt turnaround confirm our suspicion that she is both attracted by the sights she observes and repelled by them because of her strict upbringing.

The other excursions continue to emphasize the dichotomy between the world view of the Italians and that of the Joyces. At the site of the Cumaean Sibyl, another insinuating Italian guide embarrasses Katherine by placing her in the same spot where the Saracens once sacrificed women, and here once again, Mediterranean sensuality overwhelms Anglo-Saxon temperament. On the trip to the lava fields, before reaching her destination, Rossellini shows her being amazed by the large number of strolling lovers and pregnant women along the streets. Another guide there demonstrates the mystery of ionization near the lava beds, where any source of fire, such as a cigarette, produces an eruption of steam everywhere in the field. The very soil itself in Italy thus has a mysterious sense of harmony with sexual energy

Katherine Joyce as the epitome of upper-middle-class respectability. *Source*: Museum of Modern Art Film Stills Archives

Alexander flirts with an Italian girl while musicians serenade them. *Source*: Museum of Modern Art Film Stills Archives

that amazes and frightens Katherine. Later, after counting six pregnant women on a single block as she drives to the catacombs, where Italians preserve the skeletons of their beloved relatives and visit them just as Katherine would living friends, Katherine learns that the lust for life in Italy entails the acceptance of its counterpart, death.

The structure of these various visits may be said to embody the principle of repetition with variation (a structural principle that underlies many of the films in the same period by such directors as Antonioni and Fellini). It is a narrative structure guaranteed to evoke from some audiences the complaint that nothing ever really happens. This general narrative pattern is rendered with what must be described as a thoroughly impassive cinematic style, Rossellini's celebrated long takes that avoid extensive dramatic cutting in favor of the *plan-séquence*, the organization of an action in a single complex take that might normally be shot by a traditional director in a sequence of separate and shorter shots. As one English critic has rightly noted, in such takes, "Bergman's presence is central to the shot, and we look *at* her as much as *with* her."[15] To return to the example of the museum visit, then, Rossellini manages to convey, with the particular *plan-séquence* style that became his artistic signature, both a subjective sense of what it must be like to be Katherine Joyce, gazing at works of art in a museum that shock her prudish sensibilities, and a more impassive, objection vision of the psychological process taking place within his character's psyche, by containing both the art object and the reaction to it within a single complex shot.

Rossellini himself has pointed out an important difference between his technique in *Viaggio in Italia* and conventional Hollywood narrative cinema:

> Usually in the traditional cinema a scene is constructed like this: an establishing shot in which the environment is defined; the discovery of an individual in that environment; you move closer to him (medium shot); then a two-shot; a close-up; and the story begins. I proceed in a manner which is exactly opposite to that: I always begin with a close-up; then the movement of the character determines the movement of the camera. The camera does not leave the actor, and in this way the camera effects the most complex journeys.[16]

Here, Rossellini exaggerates somewhat, since *Viaggio in Italia* mixes examples of his nonconventional technique outlined above with a number of traditional transitions from long establishing shots toward more intimate portraits of the protagonists, who are followed by the camera in a complex take. Somewhat surprisingly, Rossellini employs such a conventional structure in portraying the most impressive and moving of the several tourist trips in his film: Katherine's visit to the excavation of Pompeii. Now for the first time, she is accompanied by her husband, Alexander. The couple witness the making of a plaster mold of several inhabitants of the city who were killed in the historic eruption of Vesuvius centuries earlier. The sequence begins with an extremely traditional establishing shot, a slow pan that shows us the entire sweep of Pompeii, but the traditional panoramic view of a tourist attraction develops into Rossellini's characteristically long take, as the pan continues until it comes to rest upon the men making the plaster cast. It is followed by a medium close-up of the Joyce couple and then a similar shot of the plaster mold. What they observe is the most disconcerting image in the entire film – the discovery of the remains of a couple trapped in the eruption and eternally frozen in each other's arms. It is unclear whether they were seeking solace in a moment of terror or were simply surprised while making love. No single image could be in greater contrast to the sterility and unhappiness characteristic of the Joyce couple. The scene provokes a morbid reaction from Katherine, who runs away, and the vision of the couple frozen in time seems to confirm the eventual divorce the Joyces agree to obtain. As they drive back toward Naples, they witness a religious procession that suddenly inspires them to give their marriage another chance, a surprising conclusion to a film that seemed until the final sequence to present monumental obstacles to any such reconciliation.

Rossellini's conscious exclusion of melodramatic twists or sudden devel-

The end of modern love amidst classical ruins: Alexander and Katherine visit the Roman excavations at Pompeii. *Source*: Centro sperimentale di cinematografia Photograph Archives

opments in *Viaggio in Italia*, with the exception of his surprising and puzzling reversal at the conclusion of the film, represents an effort to avoid the type of narrative typical of successful commercial films. As Rossellini remarked shortly after making the film in 1954, "I always try to be impassive. I find that whatever is astonishing, unusual and moving in men, it is precisely that great actions and great deeds come about in the same way, with the same resonance as normal everyday occurrences. I try to relate both with the same humility."[17] This impassive attitude toward the object of the camera's gaze suits perfectly Rossellini's preference for avoiding dramatic editing and its juxtaposition of contrasting shots in favor of the long take and the mobile camera. In a second interview with Rohmer and Truffaut, in which *Viaggio in Italia* was discussed as a prototype of Rossellini's style, the director declared that he could not agree with those critics and directors who felt montage in the classical sense, that associated with the work of Eisenstein, represented the essence of cinematic art:

Montage is no longer necessary. Things are there ... why manipulate them? ... The technical process is always amazing: not for me, but for

The Joyces driving in their car (a symbol of their alienation) toward yet another unsatisfying Italian experience together. *Source*: Museum of Modern Art Film Stills Archives

a lot of people. Well, it's the same thing with montage: it's a bit like the magician's hat. You put all these techniques into it and then you bring out a dove, a bunch of flowers, a carafe of water... you give it a stir and again you bring out a carafe of water, a dove, etc.... Taken in this sense at any rate, montage is something I am averse to and that I think no longer necessary.... It was probably necessary in silent films. ...And what is also important is that the camera today has become completely mobile. In the silent period it was totally immobile. In the early days using tracking shots was considered a piece of madness.[18]

Throughout the entire film, the Joyces have shielded themselves from the emotional impact of life that the more sensual and erotic Neapolitans experience quite naturally. The most important symbolic motif that underlines this theme in the film is their British car — quite out of place, with its steering wheel on the wrong side for Italy and its boring, insect-like sound — which carries the couple or Katherine on the tourist excursions with an annoying noise that Rossellini obviously employed to emphasize the car's symbolic function.[19] The car serves as a protective womb, but when Katherine and Alexander leave the car, as they both do at the excavation in Pompeii and during the religious procession concluding the film, they begin to feel the influence of the alien "toga" culture around them.

Numerous critics have objected that the sudden reconciliation taking place as a result of the religious procession is completely unmotivated and unbelievable. And it is certainly true that the dialogue, particularly as delivered by the priggish George Sanders, is excruciatingly flat:

ALEXANDER: How can they believe in that? They're like a bunch of children!
KATHERINE: Children are happy.... Alex, I don't want you to hate me. I don't want it to finish this way.
ALEXANDER: Oh, Katherine, what are you driving at? What game are you trying to play? You've never understood me, you've never even tried. And now this nonsense. What is it you want?
KATHERINE: Nothing. I despise you.[20]

Such a stilted, almost unbelievable exchange is immediately followed by perhaps the most powerful shot in the film. While the crowd in the religious procession chants "Miracle! Miracle!" Katherine is swept away and ahead of the camera by the racing multitude, with her back to Alexander and the camera, as she screams for help. Alexander comes to her assistance, and

Alexander desperately searches for Katherine in the crowd scene that closes the film. *Source*: Museum of Modern Art Film Stills Archives

Alexander and Katherine are miraculously reconciled at the end of the film.
Source: Museum of Modern Art Film Stills Archives

for the first and only time in the film, they embrace in an attempt to transcend the deadly sterility of their meaningless marriage. The banality of their dialogue (a banality I take to be intentional on the part of the director) cannot hope to capture the mystery of the moment:

ALEXANDER: Katherine, what's wrong with us? Why do we torture each other?
KATHERINE: When you say things that hurt me, I try to hurt you back, don't you see, but I can't any longer, because I love you.
ALEXANDER: Perhaps we get hurt too easily.
KATHERINE: Tell me that you love me.
ALEXANDER: Well, if I do, will you promise not to take advantage of me?
KATHERINE: Oh, yes, but I want to hear you say it.
ALEXANDER: All right, I love you.

In an interview given in 1965, Rossellini remarked that the enigmatic ending of his film should be compared to the instinctive reaction of people surprised naked. They spontaneously grasp a towel or draw closer to the people near them in an attempt to cover their nakedness.[21] We must also consider Rossellini's evaluation of the miraculous epiphany concluding the story, the Joyces' surprising embrace in the midst of the procession. Rossellini's interviewers asked if the film did not, in fact, have a "false happy ending," and Rossellini's reply, mistranslated in the often-cited *Screen* interview, was an immediate "of course, it's a very bitter film, isn't it, after all?"[22] In fact, it seems that Rossellini intended the kind of enigmatic and open-ended final sequence so typical of the works of other Italian directors of the period, especially Michelangelo Antonioni and Federico Fellini. Although his intentions may not be completely realized in the final sequence, his comments leave no doubt that the director did not see the sudden epiphany at the close of the film as the final word in the relationship of the English couple. That this is the case may also be deduced from the fact that it is not the embrace that ends the film but, instead, a rather inconsequential shot of a member of the village band, as if the director meant to undermine any obviously positive interpretation of the couple's reconciliation.

Viaggio in Italia will never become a popular film. Rossellini's avoidance of traditional dramatic construction with its increase of narrative suspense toward a resounding climax, the flat delivery of the English dialogue and the essentially antitheatrical acting style of his cast, his long takes and avoidance of climactic editing techniques, and his emphasis on minute psychological nuances in the lives of vapid and superficial protagonists will never result in box-office appeal in any commercial cinematic culture. But Rossellini's innovations in cinematic narrative, even if not always quite so original as the enthusiastic French critics of the *Cahiers du Cinéma* group claimed, nevertheless represented an important alternative to the dominant cinematic language of Hollywood. A new generation of young filmmakers applauded his efforts to transcend established narrative structures, which were all too closely linked to the dramatic conventions of traditional film and literature. Italian neorealism had largely ignored psychological realism in an attempt to show how environment shaped character during the immediate postwar period, when unemployment and the reconstruction of Italy were the most important central facts of life. Rossellini's *Viaggio in Italia* helped to move Italian cinema back toward a cinema of psychological introspection and visual symbolism where character and environment served to emphasize the newly established protagonist of modernist cinema, the isolated and alienated individual.[23]

7
Il generale Della Rovere
Commercial Success and a Reconsideration of Neorealism

In a 1970 interview, Rossellini rejected dramatization and the search for effects in the cinema as falsifications of reality. He also remarked that *Il generale Della Rovere* was a "constructed film, a professional film, and I do not make professional films, only films that we can call experimental."[1] However, in the wake of Rossellini's long string of commercially unsuccessful films, the director was desperate for financial backing, and when the critical success of his documentary on India at the Cannes Film Festival gave his tarnished reputation a breath of oxygen, Rossellini's opportunistic nature lost no time in assembling a project that would have commercial potential. Using a short story by the Italian journalist Indro Montanelli that was selected in May 1959, Rossellini and his scriptwriters (Sergio Amidei, Diego Fabbri, Piero Zuffi, and Montanelli) turned out a script in less than a month. Because Rossellini's commercial backers needed to introduce the work at the Venice Biennale in late August of that same year to guarantee a return on their investment, shooting was completed in an amazing four weeks' time. The completely edited work was presented at the end of August in Venice, where it was awarded the major festival prize, the Golden Lion Award, together with Mario Monicelli's *La grande guerra (The Great War)*. When *Il generale Della Rovere* was released commercially, it earned over 650 million lire, more than forty times the box-office receipts he had obtained with *Viaggio in Italia*, and the film cost a paltry $300,000 to make.[2] In view of Rossellini's almost self-destructive avoidance of box-office success throughout the period when his work was identified with Ingrid Bergman, such a meteoric rise to commercial and critical success represents only one of many paradoxes in his intriguing career.

Il generale Della Rovere cannot but remind the viewer of the themes of

Roma città aperta and *Paisà,* which first brought Rossellini to the attention of the entire world. Set in war-torn Genoa and Milan during 1943 around the time of the Allied landings at Anzio, when the partisans were fighting the Germans and the Italian Fascists of the Republic of Salò in the north of Italy, Rossellini's film follows the adventures of a consummate con man and gambler, Emanuele Bardone (alias Colonel Grimaldi), who makes a living by helping to save Italians arrested by the Gestapo, or by pretending to do so. For his troubles, he is paid with cash, jewels, and even packages of salami by the desperate relatives and friends of the prisoners. However, his habitual gambling and bad luck at the tables leave him constantly in need of money, and as the film opens, we discover that he has already lost the fifty thousand lire he must give to a German bureaucrat named Walter at German headquarters in Genoa in order to save the life of a client's son. By accident, Bardone meets Colonel Müller, the commander of the German garrison, on a bridge where the German's car has a flat tire. Müller is struck by the Italian's likable personality and ingratiating manner. Later, when

Bardone, the Italian con artist, meets Colonel Müller by chance and offers his assistance. *Source*: Centro sperimentale di cinematografia Photograph Archives

Desperate for cash, Bardone tries a confidence game on his old girlfriend Olga inside the brothel where she works. *Source*: Museum of Modern Art Film Stills Archives

Bardone's confidence games go sour (he makes the fatal mistake of trying to obtain money to save a man who has already been executed), he is turned in to the German authorities by the victim's wife, and he once again meets Colonel Müller, but under less-polite circumstances. However, because of Bardone's agreeable manner and his obvious cupidity, Müller offers him the choice between being executed or running a confidence game for him inside a prison in Milan. Müller had intended to capture an Italian general (the General Della Rovere of the film's title) after he had been landed on the beaches near Genoa by an Allied submarine to contact an Italian named Fabrizio, the commander of partisan forces in the Milanese area. When Müller's men intercepted the general, he was accidentally killed, frustrating

Müller's plan to use Della Rovere to ferret out the Resistance leader Fabrizio. Müller knows that Fabrizio is one of his prisoners but is unable to determine his precise identity. If Bardone masquerades as General Della Rovere, Müller can send him to the prison in the hope that Fabrizio will contact him, thereby revealing his identity to Müller. But contrary to Müller's carefully laid plans, after Bardone – alias Colonel Grimaldi, alias General Giovanni Braccioforte Della Rovere – learns the identity of the prisoner Fabrizio, he marches off with the other prisoners to his execution, refusing Müller's offer of safe passage to Switzerland and a million lire. Rather than providing the name Müller seeks, Bardone's last act before facing the firing squad is to leave the incredulous German officer with a message for his "wife," Countess Bianca Maria Della Rovere: "My last thoughts were of you – long live Italy!"[3]

Rossellini's return to the themes of *Roma città aperta* and *Paisà* in *Il generale Della Rovere* suggests to viewers a critical reconsideration of that historical period and the films that represented it. A younger generation of filmmakers following the neorealist masters – Bernardo Bertolucci, Pier Paolo Pasolini, Marco Bellocchio, Gillo Pontecorvo, the Taviani brothers – all came of age artistically during the decade following *Il generale Della Rovere,* and all of their early films deal, in some measure, with an aesthetic reconsideration of the neorealist legacy in both style and content. Rossellini's example in this film was an important guide to these young Italian directors, even though Rossellini knew few of them personally and was on far friendlier terms with the French intellectuals of the New Wave.[4] As the most important film movement or moment in Italian cinematic history, neorealism was a springboard for subsequent generations of filmmakers in Italy, and with Rossellini's revisitation of the movement that made him famous, the director once again found himself in the Italian cinematic avant-garde.

Another equally important contribution *Il generale Della Rovere* makes to Italian film history may escape the notice of anyone not thoroughly familiar with Italian film culture. Rossellini's film was one of the first of a new genre of Italian tragicomic films that examined the historical period usually associated with the neorealists in a totally ironic light untypical of the neorealist classics. In *Il generale Della Rovere,* Rossellini replaces partisan priests, Marxist political leaders, Allied liberators, and Italian guerrillas with a most unlikely protagonist – a con artist antihero. Mario Monicelli's *La grande guerra,* the film that shared the main prize at the Venice festival with Rossellini's, employs two similarly antiheroic soldiers (played by the consummate comic actors Alberto Sordi and Vittorio Gassman) to depict the disastrous Italian military defeat at the battle of Caporetto in the First World War. Only a few years later, Monicelli would produce *I compagni* (*The Organizer*, 1963), a hilarious portrayal of the rise of Italian socialism during a violent textile strike in Turin in 1890. Here, the leader of the workers' strike is a bumbling intellectual played by Marcello Mastroianni. Luigi Comencini's *Tutti a casa!* (*Everybody Home!* 1960), a title derived from the cheer of Italian soldiers when they learned of the short-lived armistice proclaimed by Marshal Badoglio on 8 September 1943 after Mussolini's fall from power, creates another antiheroic figure, an Italian officer played by Alberto Sordi who abandons his post and heads for home with his men. During a picaresque journey through a defeated Italy, the officer finally learns the meaning of brotherhood and devotion to duty and decides to join partisans fighting the Nazis. Luciano Salce's *Il federale* (*The Fascist*, 1965) employs a bumbling Ugo Tognazzi as a maniacal bureaucrat who insists upon becoming a Fascist *federale* at precisely the moment when all intelligent Fascists are abandoning their uniforms and their posts as the advancing Allied armies make membership in the party not only dangerous but futile as well.

These are only a few of the most important films of the period that approach the tragic events of the war and the Resistance in an irreverent, tragicomic manner. They and many similar works owe a debt to Rossellini's example in shifting the treatment of the Resistance from one of somewhat-pious hagiography to an image tempered by humor, critical analysis, and a healthy dose of self-deprecation. One of the common thematic strands linking all such tragicomic views of Italy's role in the Second World War is the sudden conversion of the protagonist to the "correct" ideological position at the end of the film in a startling reversal (something that characterized a number of Rossellini's earlier films, as we have already seen). Thus, Monicelli's two cowardly soldiers suddenly rebel against a Prussian officer disparaging Italian courage and die before a firing squad (much like Rossellini's Bardone); Comencini's sunshine patriot has a change of heart after witnessing German atrocities and joins the partisans; even Salce's diehard Fascist *federale* finally sees the light and gives up his lifelong ambition when the course of events finally sinks into his feeble brain.

In short, Rossellini begins a long process in the Italian cinema with *Il generale Della Rovere* that transforms the treatment of war, Resistance, fascism, and other typical neorealist subjects from an obligatory and completely tragic perspective to one tempered by the subtle laughter of the traditional Italian comic film, the *commedia all'italiana*. Although a number of leftist intellectuals would object to such a desecration of a theme they preferred to be treated with all the possible solemnity ideological purity might generate, there is no doubt that with *Il generale Della Rovere*, Rossellini initiates several important shifts in Italian cinema. On the level of content and genre, Rossellini moves the depiction of typical neorealist themes (the war, the Resistance) away from a strictly tragic tone to one that permits questioning and doubts about the nature of Italy's role in the war. Neorealist practice had transformed the Resistance into a myth; Rossellini allowed his audience to see the artifice concealed beneath the halos the saints of the Resistance wore. Within only two decades after Rossellini's pioneering example, the shift to a tragicomic vision of the Italian fascist period would produce such undisputed masterpieces as Bernardo Bertolucci's *La strategia del ragno*, Federico Fellini's *Amarcord* (1974), and Lina Wertmüller's *Pasqualino Settebellezze* (*Seven Beauties,* 1976), all of which continue the demythologization of neorealist themes. Perhaps more important, however, with his use of an uncharacteristic commercial style and a return to a reliance on the expressive powers of the professional actor (Vittorio De Sica), Rossellini reexamines the far more perplexing question of the relationship between film art and cinematic realism, an issue that lay at the heart of Italian neorealism.

Rossellini's most original neorealist film, *Paisà,* pointed to the ambiguous interrelationship between illusion and reality, fact and fiction. One only has to think of the implications of the Neapolitan sequence where the black American soldier jumps onto the puppet stage to give battle to the white Christian knights in defense of the Moorish puppets to realize that Rossellini's relationship to cinematic realism had always been a dialectical, problematic one and was never a mere search for "realism" in style and content. Thus, a philosophical problem that Rossellini only touches upon in *Paisà* becomes central to the plot of *Il generale Della Rovere.* Only if we insist on interpreting Rossellini's entire career as a single-minded quest for an equally single-minded film realism can we condemn *Il generale Della Rovere* as a betrayal of his past. And yet, a number of recent critics who admire Rossellini's most avant-garde techniques and rate *Viaggio in Italia* as his most original film (following the *Cahiers du Cinéma* critics) condemn Rossellini's commercial success out of hand. For one, the film fails because it supposedly "simulates history in an unsuccessful attempt to achieve documentary";[5] for another, it "contains barely a hint of the depth or resonance of a film like *Voyage to Italy*" and "ultimately registers as little more than a bravura piece of acting."[6]

No harm is done when critics recognize and praise innovative elements of a director's style that lack appeal to a broader, commercial audience.

But Rossellini has for too long been viewed through the somewhat eccentric lens of the *Cahiers du Cinéma* group (and their Anglo-American followers). Their perspective implicitly portrays Rossellini as a tragic and misunderstood genius who was shunned by a philistine and reactionary commercial cinema. However, Rossellini cannot very well be placed in the role of victim. He consciously decided to embark upon noncommercial projects during the course of his career and was defended in so doing by quite able critical allies in France. Later, when he left film for television, he managed to avoid commercial considerations entirely because Italian television was a state monopoly enterprise. His audiences were offered two choices. They could watch his didactic history films or turn off the television set and go to the cinema. Few directors rejecting the demands of commercial cinema have been so fortunate as Rossellini in finding such a privileged outlet on television or in receiving funding on such a massive scale.

Although commercial, mainstream cinema often rejects aesthetic innovations made at the expense of box-office success, it would be foolish to use the anticommercial qualities of most of Rossellini's films as an argument that they are, solely by virtue of their lack of popular appeal, masterpieces. Lack of popular appeal does not, per se, guarantee the quality of a work of art, nor does popularity at the box office negate artistic genius. With *Il generale Della Rovere*, Rossellini proved that he could produce a money-making movie that also made a serious and original artistic statement about the relationship of fact and fiction in the cinema, and the praiseworthy features of this film are by no means diminished because of its success with international audiences.

We have already seen how Rossellini's original and antirhetorical use of Hollywood actors Ingrid Bergman and George Sanders in *Viaggio in Italia* (not to mention a similar method in each of his films in which Ingrid Bergman performed) represented an implicit critique of traditional Hollywood acting conventions. In *Viaggio in Italia,* for example, Rossellini places veteran performers in a strange and unfamiliar environment and derives original aesthetic results precisely because he elicits un-Hollywood-like acting performances, with leaden, one-dimensional, and surprisingly inarticulate dialogue, from consummate Hollywood actors accustomed to virtuoso acting. In a real sense, Rossellini turns Sanders and Bergman into nonprofessional actors (if professional acting is to be understood as reflecting the conventional Hollywood acting codes for melodrama), whose mannerisms on the screen cannot help but recall the self-consciously uncomfortable (and therefore believable) performances Rossellini achieved with his nonprofessionals in *Paisà*.

In *Il generale Della Rovere*, Rossellini makes another experiment with acting that has interesting theoretical implications. Earlier, in *Roma città aperta*, he had cast Aldo Fabrizi, a vaudeville comedian, as the brilliantly tragicomic figure of Don Pietro, the partisan priest. With De Sica cast as a swindler masquerading as an Italian general, Rossellini effects a similar transformation by assigning Italy's most famous light comedian in the fascist period and in the 1950s the role of a heroic figure. To appreciate how much Rossellini upset the expectations of European audiences (who knew De Sica as an actor in addition to his contributions as a director), we must consider De Sica's public persona and his typecasting as an Italian star.

U.S. critics and audiences identify De Sica primarily as the director of classic neorealist films about unemployment (*Ladri di biciclette*), old age (*Umberto D.*, 1951), or orphans without families in the rubble of postwar Italy (*Sciuscià [Shoeshine]*, 1946), but Italian audiences knew De Sica best as an actor whose personality was very much like that of the confidence man in Rossellini's film. Like the false General Della Rovere, De Sica's favorite pastime was gambling, and there is some evidence to support the often-voiced critical opinion of his detractors that not a few of De Sica's post-neorealist films were made solely to cover his gambling debts. For an audience knowledgeable about De Sica's personal life – and in Italy, he had been the object of gossip columns in film magazines since his debut in the light comedies of the 1930s – seeing De Sica in the role of an inveterate gambler would have heightened the sense of realism in the film. Rossellini might be seen here as returning to neorealist principles of casting. The personality of the real individual Vittorio De Sica – inveterate gambler and likable lady's man – matched the role embodied in General Della Rovere, just as the protagonist of De Sica's *Ladri di biciclette* was chosen for the part because his actual past experience and physical appearance suggested the kind of worker he was to play in the film.

If we consider the type of roles associated with De Sica, however – those with Mario Camerini during the 1930s that typecast him as a romantic leading man in light comedies – the relationship between De Sica and General Della Rovere can be viewed from another perspective. De Sica's brilliant acting career may be said to have been formed by several key films in the 1930s which impressed upon his public persona a particular kind of role that was forever after identified with him on the screen. In Mario Camerini's *Gli uomini, che mascalzoni!* De Sica plays Bruno, a poor chauffeur, who tries to win the favors of a beautiful but poor young girl by pretending to be a wealthy sophisticate. In Baldassare Negroni's *Due cuori felici* (*Two Happy Hearts*, 1932), De Sica plays Mr. Brown, a wealthy U.S. industrialist

Bardone, now playing the role of the Resistance hero General Della Rovere, inside the prison after his torture. *Source*: Museum of Modern Art Film Stills Archives

who owns the L. Thomas Brown Automobile Company and who speaks English (with an amazing American accent) as well as an amusing Americanized Italian; when he visits his Italian representative, Brown mistakes a lowly secretary for the representative's wife and falls in love with her. In Mario Camerini's *Darò un milione* (*I'd Give a Million*, 1935), a film that inspired a Hollywood remake, De Sica plays a millionaire named Gold who pretends to be poor and promises to give a million lire to any person who performs a spontaneous and unselfish act of kindness toward him. And finally, in Camerini's *Il Signor Max* (*Mr. Max*, 1937), perhaps the most important of all such films and certainly the one that established De Sica's typecasting for decades in light comedies, De Sica plays a poor newspaper vendor masquerading as a rich bon vivant in the fashionable circles of aristocratic Rome. In each of these works, as well as in a number of others starring De Sica, role playing in society is the film's major theme. In each case, the protagonist played by De Sica is a thoroughly likable, comic figure – a combination of the French Maurice Chevalier (De Sica sings and dances) and Hollywood's Cary Grant – who moves back and forth between a false persona he assumes in society (usually to romance a beautiful woman) and his authentic, more humble, and more likable personality.[7]

Rossellini did not choose De Sica to play General Della Rovere merely to have a commercially viable actor in his cast, as most recent assessments of the film suggest. Rather, he had determined to exploit De Sica's type-casting as an actor completely identified with role playing by the Italian public. By foregrounding the problematic style and quality of De Sica's acting performance in the film, Rossellini introduces a metacinematic dimension to *Il generale Della Rovere*. His emphasis on the acting style of his protagonist is but one of many elements in the film that call attention to its enigmatic theme of the interplay between reality and illusion, fact and fiction. Rossellini offers us two possible explanations for De Sica's casting: a "neorealist" one that identifies De Sica's authentic personality with the character he portrays on the screen and a "commercial" one that exploits

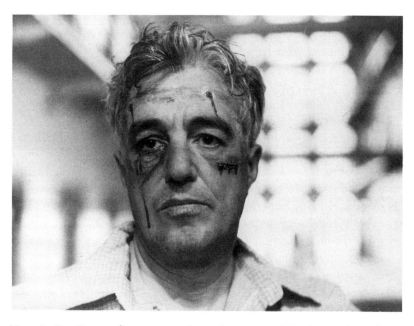

Vittorio De Sica made up to recall another tortured Resistance hero from Rossellini's neorealist past, Manfredi of *Roma città aperta*. *Source*: Centro sperimentale di cinematografia Photograph Archives

De Sica's completely "artificial" and conventional cinematic casting as a comic stereotype.

By making De Sica his reluctant hero, Rossellini invites a comparison with the neorealist vision of an earlier period. Rossellini's neorealist films on the war view Germans as unequivocally evil and Italians as heroic but innocent victims, struggling to free their country. Moral issues were black or white, rarely clouded by gray areas of doubt or ambivalence (such as considering Italian complicity with the Germans). By 1959, Rossellini's view of the events that took place in 1943 reflects an ironic awareness that the sacrifices made during the Resistance had not always led to the springtime in Italy Francesco of *Roma città aperta* fervently believed was on the horizon. What first strikes the viewer of *Il generale Della Rovere* is not only the ambivalence of the moral world of the film, when compared with the Manichaean clash of good and evil in *Roma città aperta* or *Paisà,* but also the drastically constricted range of moral issues involved. Bardone refuses to reveal the identity of the Resistance leader in the prison to Müller not merely because he safeguards vital information (as did Manfredi and Don Pietro). Instead, there is the clear suggestion that Bardone does so in order to create a perfect role in which art and life intertwine. Only by going to his death as the general can Bardone produce the perfect confidence game, swindling not only Müller but even the general's wife in the process. Moreover, Fabrizio, the Resistance leader whom Bardone refuses to identify, is already in the Germans' clutches and is scheduled to be shot with the group after Bardone. Existential questions of personal identity and role playing in society thus vie with more traditional values of personal bravery and patriotism in Rossellini's critical revisitation of the Resistance experience.

This narrowed moral focus is evident from Rossellini's detailed presentation of Bardone, which stresses the themes of deception and illusion. Rossellini concentrates less upon the political implications of the events he portrays than upon the strange transformation in Bardone's character that takes place as the role he performs begins to reshape his personality. In one memorable scene during an air raid, Bardone calms the Italian prisoners in the restricted political section of the jail, where the inmates are not permitted to seek refuge in the bomb shelters even during major air raids. Overcoming his own terror and cowardice, Bardone emerges from his cell and declaims a brave speech: "Calm, calm, show these scum that you are free men."[8] His courageous words immediately quiet the men, who believe the confidence man to be an authentic hero and leader of the Resistance. But Rossellini also permits us to witness Bardone's terror before and after the speech, revealing it to be a sham, an illusion deceiving the terrified prisoners. Bardone is then tortured by Müller to bolster his credibility with the other prisoners, but the torture has a surprising effect, causing Bardone to embrace in earnest a role Müller expects him only to feign. Soon, he is caught up in the gripping personal drama of the man he impersonates, when he receives letters from the general's wife with emotionally moving pictures of their children. Gradually, Bardone is transformed from a shallow swindler into an admirable figure worthy of the role he impersonates. His invented persona eventually dominates his own faulty character, and Bardone ultimately becomes the man he initially only pretended to be. Declaring that dying for a just cause is preferable to dying for no cause at all, Bardone refuses to reveal Fabrizio's identity. His execution is the ultimate triumph of the con artist, his final and most impressive swindle. But there is something quite puzzling about this histrionic gesture. Müller's reaction mirrors our own, for Bardone's act represents an action we would consider credible for even an instant only because of a brilliant performance by a gifted actor. And therein lies the rub, for Rossellini presents a self-consciously artificial performance, rendered in an exaggerated style by one of Italy's greatest actors, that completely nullifies any pretense to a real depiction of the historical past.

De Sica's histrionic acting abilities represent the most obvious and explicit emphasis upon the *artifice* in Rossellini's film, but there are numerous other stylistic elements in the work that highlight to the attentive viewer how Rossellini's "realistic" portrait of 1943 ultimately depends entirely upon cinematic fabrication. The director's presence is apparent in the film in a number of ways. One of the most surprising is a cameo appearance by Rossellini himself in a crowd of Italians anxiously waiting at German headquarters in Genoa.[9] We expect such an in-joke from a superb commercial showman such as Alfred Hitchcock, but a cameo appearance in a "realistic" film by Rossellini has quite a different impact upon the audience. Other, more significant details of the film's style emphasize its artifice even more plainly. For the first time in his career, Rossellini employs the special zoom lens known as the Pancinor.[10] It is used sparingly but effectively during the important bombardment scene inside the prison that introduces De Sica's most histrionic speech. This Pancinor lens becomes increasingly important in Rossellini's later works and will be discussed further in Chapter 8. Here it suffices to note the zoom's most obvious characteristic: its obtrusiveness.[11] Employing the zoom during De Sica's dramatic speech to the other prisoners emphasizes the camera and, therefore, foregrounds the artifice of the scene being reproduced.

We have already noted that the film was made in record time, practically entirely within a studio. The result of this studio production stands in marked contrast to the much more believable exteriors and interiors of Rossellini's neorealist trilogy. Some of the sets he built are so mannered (such as the bridge on which Colonel Müller's car has a flat tire, providing the occasion for meeting Bardone) that they seem taken from a German expressionist film instead of a work that supposedly pays homage to Italian neorealism. The obviously artificial lighting inside the studio settings (again, most noticeable in the bombardment sequence) increases our lack of confidence in the physical reality of what we are shown on the screen. It is all so clearly constructed in the dream factory of Cinecittà.

Rossellini quite frequently employs the wipe, a transitional device used between scenes that practically demands to be noticed. Other special effects likewise reinforce the emphasis on film illusion over film realism. In one interesting scene, partisans meet near the Duomo, in the center of Milan, in winter, but the snow on the ground and the church in the background are patently produced by a rear projection. It seems inconceivable that Rossellini could not have done a more convincing job of deceiving the audience if that had been his intention, but it was precisely the artificiality of the scene he wished to convey. The foregrounding of the cinematic artifice behind the representation of the "reality" of the events depicted is perhaps best achieved in the climatic conclusion of the film, when Bardone is executed against a wall. Behind the dead partisans is what purports to be the skyline of the city of Milan. But once again, a closer look reveals a painted canvas backdrop so obviously contrived that it is impossible to imagine it seems so false by accident.

Rossellini's Emanuele Bardone (alias General Della Rovere) resembles a Pirandellian character at the end of the film. He reminds the viewer familiar with Pirandello's theater of the tragicomic figure Enrico IV in the play of the same name, a man who consciously assumes the identity of another historical figure and finds himself trapped in that role forever. The foregrounding of the role of the actor and the problematic treatment of "real" versus "false" identity in *Il generale Della Rovere* provide a metacinematic twist to the narrative storyline that displays, in one critic's words, Rossellini's "acceptance of cinematic artifice – role playing, the assumption of disguise – as a way toward moral truth."[12] As we shall discover in the next chapter, which is devoted to Rossellini's cinematic portrait of Louis XIV, the puzzling interrelationships between reality and appearance, mask and face, and disguise and true identity will give Rossellini a key to unlock the enigmatic motivations of the French monarch's personality.

8

La prise de pouvoir par Louis XIV

Toward a Didactic Cinema for Television

Between the time Rossellini achieved commercial success with *Il generale Della Rovere,* which he had not enjoyed since the release of his early neo-realist classics, and the making of *La prise de pouvoir par Louis XIV* for French television, he underwent a major shift in his thinking about the cinema. As early as 1961 in an essay entitled "Audiovisual Means of Communication and Man in a Scientific and Industrial Society," Rossellini argued, displaying his habitual naiveté, that traditional cinema, following the economic model encouraged by Hollywood, fostered a homogenized mass culture that hindered independent, rational thought, whereas television could provide a democratic diffusion of culture to large, commercial audiences.[1] In an often-cited interview with *Cahiers du Cinéma* in the following year, Rossellini made an important distinction to which he referred constantly when discussing the didactic potential of television. He rejected the concept of "education" (since even the word's etymology implied conditioning, guiding, directing, and ultimately coercing the person involved in the "lesson") in favor of what he preferred to call "information" or "instruction" that would allow the "student" to make his or her own choices.[2] In a subsequent *Cahiers du Cinéma* interview in 1963, Rossellini explained his rejection of commercial cinema but also attacked proponents of cinema verité, who proposed rejecting artistic interpretation in noncommercial film-making. For Rossellini, moral choices and artistic interpretation were not antithetical to the goal of uncovering truth or reality that his rejection of commercial fictional cinema implied.[3] In 1965, in an essay entitled "To Defend the Hope That Is within Each of Us," Rossellini again spelled out his reasons for abandoning the commercial cinema, which in his opinion had become part of the political or ideological structure in contemporary society that served to mystify rather than to inform and improve humanity, perverting with the corruption of propaganda the cinema's didactic potential.[4]

Although Rossellini himself made some of the first postwar films treating the classic existential themes of alienation and lack of communication between human beings, particularly in the Bergman era, he now attacked intellectuals who had only such negative portraits to paint for their publics:

> We have to have the courage to admit that in the past hundred years all art has been reduced to complaints. An artist is lesser or greater depending on how much he complains. They call it protest (*denuncia*). The fact is that it's complaining, because if it were protest it would be carried out differently, more aggressively. . . . But this eternal moaning and protesting about how much is wrong is something quite different. . . . Now, the world has a right to expect something of intellectuals, and artists in particular. If the artist can't in some sense act as a guide to point the way, if he is unable to take his bearings and say, "today, at this point in time, these are our horizons," then the function of the artist disappears. . . . I think the artist has a very definite function in this world – it is to clarify things.[5]

Rossellini's clear preference for a didactic cinema may also be seen in a document known as Rossellini's Manifesto. Although it was signed by a number of younger Italian critics and directors (including Bernardo Bertolucci, Adriano Aprà, Tinto Brass, and Vittorio Cottafavi), it is clear that the document bears the stamp of Rossellini's thinking on the role of the cinema in contemporary society, for it castigates contemporary art, and the cinema in particular, for refusing to be inspired by the enormous advances in science and technology that have occurred since the eighteenth century:

> We work in the cinema and in television, and we intend to make films and programs to help man to recognize the actual horizons of his world. We want to show, in an interesting but scientifically correct way, down to the smallest details, everything that art, or the cultural products distributed by the audio-visual media, have so far failed to show – things they have, still worse, ridiculed and abused. We wish, again, to present man with the guide-lines of his own history, and depict drama, comedy and satire, the struggles, the experiences and the psychology of the people who have made the world what it is

today, making it a criterion to fuse together entertainment, information and culture.[6]

Much of what Rossellini wrote or said in these various essays and interviews makes him sound like typical leftist intellectuals of the period, who rejected the commercial cinema because of its corruption by American values and its illusionist perspective. But Rossellini comes to such conclusions from a completely different point of view. This is made clear by his attack on intellectuals and artists he derisively labels "whiners" about alienation (and these individuals can only be identified with the Left). Moreover, unlike leftist intellectuals and artists who had a Marxist ideology to substitute for the so-called capitalist ideology that was supposedly embodied in commercial cinema, Rossellini rejected the idea of ideology altogether and believed in the possibility of intellectual neutrality, of presenting facts without a completely biased point of view. In yet another interview with *Cahiers du Cinéma* in 1965, Rossellini was asked if he believed in an ideology as a hypothesis upon which to construct a film, such as Marxism as a means of historical knowledge. His negative reply was unequivocal: "No, it is necessary to know things outside any ideology. Every ideology is a prism."[7] When pressed by the interviewers from *Cahiers* (who clearly did not agree with Rossellini's viewpoint, for they represented the quintessential French leftist intellectual), Rossellini insisted that he really believed in objectivity, in the possibility of divulging information about the past without the blinders of ideologies. Rossellini's belief marks him, in the terminology of contemporary debate about political "correctness," as a hopeless reactionary, since many of the politically correct in the academic community reject the very notion of objectivity that Rossellini espoused as itself an ideologically vitiated concept.

Rossellini's aversion to fashionable critical ideologies is most apparent in an interview he gave to two U.S. critics in 1974, the title of which is changed, significantly, to "Against Aesthetic Theories" in the Italian collection of his writings, *Il mio metodo*.[8] Many leftist critics at the time favored the aesthetic theories identified with Bertolt Brecht and the application of Brechtian views on "distanciating" effects in the theater to the cinema, following the example of Jean-Luc Godard. A number of critics attempted to link Rossellini to Brechtian aesthetics not only because of the particular style of certain of his films (for example, *Viaggio in Italia* and *La prise de pouvoir par Louis XIV*) but also because Rossellini had clearly influenced Godard and was therefore, in the eyes of these critics who canonized everything Godard had done or said, an auteur to be redeemed, especially since he was as adamant in rejecting commercial cinema at the time as were the followers of Brecht and Godard. Yet, in the 1974 interview, Rossellini is clearly not interested in the American critics' attempts to link the nondramatic and flat dialogue of *La prise de pouvoir par Louis XIV* to theories associated with Brecht or Godard, or the narrative structure of his film about the French monarch to Brecht's play *Galileo*. Rossellini can only remark in a bemused manner that he sees no point in giving value to one kind of work by comparing it with one of an entirely different sort. In spite of the director's own rejection of such analogies, comparisons of Rossellini with Brecht and Godard were in large measure responsible for the renewed critical respectability of Rossellini during the last decade of his life.[9]

Of Rossellini's many films made for television, only *La prise de pouvoir par Louis XIV* can be considered a truly great and original work. And yet this single film may well justify Rossellini's many and sometimes exaggerated claims that television film could rival the quality of film produced for the traditional cinema. Almost every incident depicted in the film, as well as most of the dialogue, comes directly from historical documents of the period. The scholarly accuracy of the film owes much to the fact that the French historian Philippe Erlanger's biography of Louis XIV served as the basis for the film and Erlanger himself assisted Rossellini in writing the screenplay. The plot of the film is economical and deceptively simple and does not cover the entire reign of the French monarch but only his seizure of power upon the death of Cardinal Mazarin, the French prime minister.

Besides the film's remarkable concentration of historical information within such a brief span of historical time, the production of the film for French television was a triumph of Rossellini's technological ingenuity. With only 100 million lire (about $130,000 at the prevailing exchange rates) with which to work, Rossellini shot the entire film in less than a month, working part of each day, since labor problems prohibited more than five and one-half hours of work by the television crew daily. Postproduction editing was cut to the barest minimum, thanks in part to Rossellini's expertise at setting up shots rapidly, but particularly to a technical innovation Rossellini had introduced in *Il generale Della Rovere*, his Pancinor zoom lens. With Rossellini's special zoom lens, the director saved time by practically eliminating tracking shots (and the time-consuming preparation of such shots on the set), in effect editing sequences within long takes made with the zoom lens. Thus, the *plan-séquence* style emphasizing long takes from Rossellini's earlier career was now fitted in a perfect marriage to the new technological advance of the Pancinor lens. But Rossellini also realized that television required a greater closeness or intimacy between the action on the screen and the audience than even his new zoom lens could produce. He resolved this problem by putting the new zoom lens and camera on a dolly that had three to four meters of track in front of the camera. Actors could thus move freely on the set, and Rossellini could shift easily between long or medium shots of the entire set to medium close-ups or close-ups with the zoom. The problem of an actor covering up another actor while moving about on the set was resolved by the few meters of track in front of the camera, which permitted Rossellini to adjust his camera ever so slightly (in a manner that is usually imperceptible on the screen) to avoid such inconveniences. Moreover, Rossellini worked out by himself an ingenious remote control system on the zoom lens that allowed him to manipulate the lens from almost anywhere on the set.[10]

An equally important technical advance allowed Rossellini to pursue his vision of a true and historically accurate portrait of the distant past. Crucial to Rossellini's economical reconstruction of the past in his television films was his use of a modified version of the Schüfftan process. Eugen Schüfftan had invented this famous approach to special effects in the early years of the cinema, and it was employed successfully in a number of major German expressionist works, such as Fritz Lang's *Metropolis* (1926). This process is a means of combining live action with mirror-reflected images of paintings or scale models (or the opposite) by removing parts of the reflective coating on the mirror surface. Rossellini modified the mirrors by using an innovative spray made of glucose and aluminum salt that was applied to clear glass to produce a transparent mirror; he then combined an image before the camera with an image reflected by the mirror behind the camera.

The Schüfftan process enabled the director to re-create complex scenes from the past without much expense. In *La prise de pouvoir par Louis XIV*, for example, the Schüfftan process creates the illusion that Rossellini is actually present during the construction of the palace of Versailles. Employing the usual mattes and mirrors, we are first shown what seems to be hundreds of workmen captured in a long shot, toiling upon the scaffolding as if they were faceless ants. An abrupt cut from this special effect to the actual façade of the completed palace creates a startling and unforgettable impact upon the viewer, emphasizing the grandeur and even the megalomania of the French monarch's architectural schemes. A recent Italian book on Rossellini's cinema by Fernaldo Di Giammateo contains a chapter devoted to Rossellini's television films, and its subtitle is "A Mirror and A Zoom, the Language of Television," underlining the crucial role that both the Schüfftan process and the Pancinor zoom lens played in Rossellini's work for television.[11]

La prise de pouvoir par Louis XIV represents an original twist in the genre of the historical costume film, a genre extremely popular during the 1960s in the commercial cinema of both Hollywood and Italy. Not surprisingly, Rossellini's treatment of the seizure of power by Louis XIV, although shot with the traditional costumes one expects from a traditional historical film, made important changes in the genre. Rossellini had two different models being produced practically under his nose at Cinecittà. One model was the Hollywood historical epic – such as Joseph Mankiewicz's Cleopatra (1963), starring Elizabeth Taylor and Richard Burton, being shot at Rome's Cinecittà, and Anthony Mann's The Fall of the Roman Empire (1964), filmed in Spain. Such grandiose films enjoyed enormous budgets and casts of internationally recognized stars and took cavalier liberties with history, usually embellishing fact with romanticized fictional details that would appeal to the commercial market. Some measure of the distance between Rossellini's historical costume drama and Mankiewicz's may be seen in the budget alone: Rossellini's entire film cost approximately what Elizabeth Taylor's jewels, wigs, and costumes cost (about $130,000); Cleopatra's dramatic entrance into the city of Rome cost a half-million dollars to film, about four times what it cost Rossellini to make his entire film![12] Another and more specifically Italian version of the historical costume film was the so-called peplum film, which reached the height of its international popularity between 1957 and 1964, when 10% of Italian film production during this period (about 170 films) was devoted to these "neomythological" films set vaguely in classical antiquity or in a distant but indeterminate past time and populated by buxom and inarticulate damsels in distress as well as by heroic musclemen. Aimed primarily at grade B movie theaters in Italy and the Third World, but eventually reaching even American television in unintentionally hilarious and badly dubbed versions, such potboilers abandoned even the slightest pretension to historical accuracy. One of the genre's most popular characters, a strongman named Maciste associated with the Carthaginian Wars of classical antiquity, could be situated at the court of the Russian czars or that of Ghengis Khan, and he might even confront Zorro, while the Biblical hero Samson might find himself in the kingdom of the Incas![13] Directors of great talent, such as Vittorio Cottafavi (La vendetta di Ercole [The Revenge of Hercules], 1960) and Sergio Leone (Il colosso di Rodi [The Colossus of Rhodes], 1960), worked in this genre, but almost everything about the peplum film was antithetical to Rossellini's purposes in his didactic historical films for television.

Rossellini's major transformation of the historical genre film emptied the story of its traditional swashbuckling or romantic subject matter. In the place of such narrative elements that embrace a melodramatic storyline, Rossellini substituted an intellectual content largely made up of abstract ideas that fostered the director's didactic goals. Rossellini's view of human history depends on an inherent theory of increasing rationality within the evolution of humanity, and his films privilege the place of individual historical protagonists and ideas over social and economic processes. Ultimately, Rossellini subscribes to the "great man" theory of history, the view that a single protagonist placed at a crucial crossroads in history can alter forever the course of events. Individualism is thus at the core of his vision of human history, and it is therefore difficult to understand how so many film critics could have seriously advanced a view of Rossellini as an implicitly Marxist thinker whose didactic films reflected not only Brechtian aesthetic principles but also a Marxist economic theory of history. Nothing could be farther from a Marxist theory of history than Rossellini's foregrounding of the role of ideas and individuals in history rather than viewing them as superstructural reflections of more fundamental economic conditions in society.[14]

Although Rossellini drastically alters the content of the historical costume film in *La prise de pouvoir par Louis XIV* by shifting attention from adventure and romance to the history of ideas and the impact of a single great protagonist, he does not completely reject the concept of spectacle inherent in the Hollywood and peplum versions of history. On the contrary, while retaining a scrupulous respect for historical fact and accuracy, Rossellini elevates the principle of spectacle to a philosophical level, demonstrating to his television audience that the French monarch's historical import lay precisely in his understanding of the power of spectacle and ritual over his courtiers and subjects. In many respects, Rossellini's television film continues the Pirandellian concept of role playing the director employed in *Il generale Della Rovere*, revealing the social masks disguising the exercise of political power and the dynamic tensions between reality and appearance that constituted the dominant theme of Rossellini's reconsideration of the Resistance.

Rossellini's concentration on the interplay of appearance and reality is set against the film's emphasis of material things and sensations. This is immediately clear in the second major sequence of the film, the medical examination of Cardinal Mazarin, whose death launches Louis XIV upon his path to power. Everything about the scene underlines the physical senses. The extremely long sequence is shot with only five (brilliant) shots, employing the Pancinor zoom and the long take in perfect harmony. An initial shot shows us two new doctors entering the scene; one sniffs the oppressive odor of the dying man. In a second shot, the doctors stand at the bedside of Mazarin, again checking the patient's sweat and sniffing it repeatedly in a medium close-up. The third and fourth shots are even longer than the others. In the third, which begins with the camera facing the bed, the doctors all move to the side of the room to examine the cardinal's feces, again sniffing them; then the doctors discuss the amount of blood in the human body, declaring that they can bleed Mazarin of almost all of it without doing harm. Furthermore, they cite popular adages in defense of their opinions, such as "The more one removes foul water, the purer the well," and "The more a mother nurses, the better the milk."[15] An equally complicated fourth shot begins on one side of the bed as a bedpan for the bleeding is requested; the bedpan is delivered and the camera follows the doctors left, then right, and finally zooms onto the cardinal as he is picked up and carried to a chair, where the zoom moves out again; the zoom then moves in to the doctor holding the cardinal's foot, where the blood will be removed, but as the camera pans to the right to capture the doctors' consultations, we hear the patient's cry on the sound track; the camera then pans back to show the doctors examining the blood and assuring the patient that they will do everything possible to cure him; finally the camera pans left. Rossellini cuts and delivers the fifth and final shot of the doctors as they leave the room.

An enormous amount of precious information is delivered by these five brilliantly conceived shots. In the first place, as one critic has noted, the scene presents the audience with a didactic lesson in seventeenth-century science, a science based on material facts.[16] The material facts of the epoch strike us as bizarre (such as the medicinal use of rhubarb and the inquisitive nostrils of the doctors). But the most important aspect of Rossellini's presentation, and one that is too often overlooked in an emphasis on his supposed "materialist" mise-en-scène, is that the doctors' explicit attention to material facts actually results in a concentration on false appearances and provides only useless "cures," such as bleeding, which actually harm the patient. Appearances are deceptive in science, and they will prove to be even more so in human affairs as Louis seizes power.

Rossellini portrays the French monarch as a supreme showman, as the creator of a spectacle that generates political power by manipulating political appearances masking political realities. We see a hint of this theme when, on his deathbed, Cardinal Mazarin refuses to receive his monarch until he has applied the proper amount of rouge to his fading cheeks. Power brokers are actors, Rossellini tells us with this significant detail, and the court of

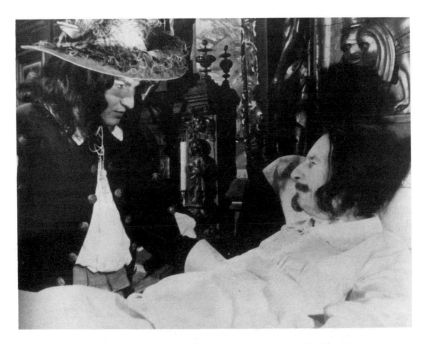

The young monarch visits Cardinal Mazarin on his deathbed before assuming full power. *Source*: Museum of Modern Art Film Stills Archives

Versailles is a stage upon which roles are being played. With the death of Mazarin and the arrival of the young monarch Louis XIV, one consummate actor makes way for another rising "star." Kingship requires a mastery of symbolic ritual, not a belief in the ritual's substance. Louis mumbles his prayers only because hypocritical public respect for religion is expected of a pious monarch; his wife claps her hands as if at the theater to signify that Louis has fulfilled his husbandly "duties"; Louis publicly refuses to accept Mazarin's legacy of sixteen million francs because he does not wish to acknowledge that the king of France can owe a debt to a commoner (and a foreigner from Italy, as well), but in private he accepts the legacy when he is assured that its source will remain a secret. The essence of the monarch rests upon the public persona of the Sun King, an assumed mask beneath which the private personality of the man Louis must never be revealed.

Rossellini's most brilliant invention in this film is to employ a concrete metaphor – the ridiculous costumes Louis required his courtiers to wear in his presence at court – as a means of visualizing the role playing behind political power. Rossellini's presentation of fashion at the court is developed

Jean-Marie Patte in the role of Louis XIV, one of Rossellini's most successful nonprofessional casting choices. *Source*: Museum of Modern Art Film Stills Archives

in the most important scene in the film, that wherein Louis explains to his master tailor exactly how he wishes his court to dress. According to Louis, Fouquet (his superintendent of finances, whom Louis has arrested in order to avoid a threat to his absolute power) had realized a single truth. Men are governed by appearances and not by the nature of things. Louis will require all his courtiers to dress in an extravagant fashion so that a single costume will cost the average nobleman a year's revenue. In fact, the more ridiculous the fashion, the more useful it will be to Louis, who plans to make the nobility dependent upon him in every respect – from their finances to their clothes. After delivering the "theory" of Louis's role playing, Rossellini then creates a practical demonstration of its effectiveness in a scene depicting the king's arrival at court in his sumptuous costume, surrounded by courtiers dressed in the same implausible manner. Louis has summoned a former adversary, a nobleman named Monsieur de Vardes, back to Versailles and once again into his good graces, but when de Vardes appears, he lacks the ridiculous costume that is de rigueur at Louis's court. He immediately apologizes for his faux pas, unwittingly falling into the monarch's cleverly laid trap. From the moment the nobleman accepts the costume of a courtier, he will be forced to play the role that accompanies it on a theatrical stage dominated by a single actor – the Sun King.

The concept of politics as pure spectacle takes on grandiose proportions during the famous banquet sequence, which, according to some sources, was shot by Rossellini's son Renzo and not the master himself. The sequence opens with a slow zoom in on Louis, dressed in his fancy costume and seated upon a raised platform, in a setting that is clearly a cross between a stage production and a religious ritual. The dozens of courses prepared by obsequious servants and served by various courtiers – the king's brother hands Louis one kind of food, while the noble musketeers of D'Artagnan are reduced to escorting the king's roast suckling pig to the table – underscore the fact that the meal is not primarily to provide nourishment but is a spectacle for the court. Finally, as Rossellini zooms out away from the king, we realize that a crowd of courtiers has been observing the king all the while, exactly as they would watch a dramatic play or a lyric opera.

The role playing of Louis is again highlighted quite effectively in the final scene of the film, which portrays the king, almost crushed by the weight of his ludicrous garments, retiring to the privacy of his chambers. Now, for a brief moment, the role player is off the stage and can revert to his true personality. Louis has seized power by transforming life into spectacle, but in the process he has assumed a role essentially devoid of intellectual or moral substance. This is evident from the slow, clumsy manner in which the king removes first his hat, then his gloves, and in rapid succession his sword, wig, sash, medals, lace, and finally his vest. In the process, he reveals himself to be a diminutive, rather pathetic individual, a consummate confidence man not unlike Bardone of *Il generale Della Rovere*. But Bardone had transcended his meaningless existence as a petty con artist by a virtuoso performance as a false (but credible) hero. Here, Rossellini achieves quite the opposite with his final depiction of Louis XIV. He deflates the Sun King's stature just as he had exalted Bardone with his execution. Even though the consequences of Louis's role playing are of more moment than Bardone's masquerade, there is no doubt that Rossellini finds Bardone's "performance" more admirable than that of the French monarch.

Behind Rossellini's conception of political power as a role-playing game of manipulating appearances and realities lie the sometimes-cynical observations on political behavior contained in Niccolò Machiavelli's classic treatise on the nature of the political ruler, *The Prince*, which was extremely popular in seventeenth-century France and was, of course, well known to Rossellini. In Chapter 18 ("How a Prince Should Keep His Word"), Machiavelli makes the following pronouncement, which defines the essence of Louis's behavior:

> A prince, therefore, must be very careful never to let anything slip from his lips which is not full of the five qualities mentioned above: he should appear ... to be all mercy, all faithfulness, all integrity, all kindness, all religion. And there is nothing more necessary than to seem to possess this last quality. And men in general judge more by their eyes than their hands; for everyone can see but few can feel. Everyone sees what you seem to be, few touch upon what you are, and those few do not dare to contradict the opinion of the many who have the majesty of the state to defend them; and in the actions of all men, and especially of princes, where there is no impartial arbiter, one must consider the final result. Let a prince therefore act to conquer and to maintain the state; his methods will always be judged honorable and will be praised by all; for ordinary people are always deceived by appearances and by the outcome of a thing; and in the world there is nothing but ordinary people; and there is no room for the few, while the many have a place to lean on.[17]

Although some recent critics have tried to explicate the genesis of Rossellini's *La prise de pouvoir par Louis XIV* by attributing to Rossellini aesthetic theories he never espoused (those of Brecht or Godard), it is clear that Rossellini found inspiration in Machiavelli's influential political treatise on the nature of the prince. Machiavelli's concept of politics as a shell game operated by a skillful confidence man at the expense of the foolish masses who mistake appearances for realities is ultimately the source for Rossellini's interpretation of the seventeenth-century French monarchy. His brilliant decision to adopt a metaphoric view of costume as a mirror of this political concept gave Rossellini an effective means of portraying his ideas in concrete, visual form, and such a simple solution to the complex question of providing a general interpretation of Louis's seizure of power also could be represented with a minimum of cost in what was an extremely low budget television film.

Machiavelli most certainly provides the intellectual focus for Rossellini's interpretation of Louis XIV, but film critics and historians have ignored the most obvious source of the film's simple but highly concentrated storyline: the French classical theater of Pierre de Corneille and Jean Racine, which was the glory of the very period Rossellini depicted in the film. Every critic writing on Rossellini's film remarks on the incredible economy with which the director concentrates on a single moment in Louis's career. In the words of one interpreter of the film, Rossellini's genius was to "see in every detail a reflection of the whole, to see in every gesture a sign of the times."[18] Restricting the action but expanding the dramatic effect of only a few key events is the essence of French classical tragedy, which may be contrasted to the luxuriant abundance and diversity of Shakespearean drama. One example may suffice to demonstrate the similarity in dramatic construction between the French theatrical works and Rossellini's film. Racine was inspired by a source in Tacitus to present the character of Nero, the Roman emperor. In his play *Brittanicus* he drastically restricts the possible narrative material on Nero to a single moment in his life: Nero's decision to murder his stepbrother Britannicus and tear himself away from the oppressive influence of his mother, the empress Agrippina. The author states in the preface to his tragedy that he wished to portray not the mature and totally depraved tyrant the entire world already knew but the "budding monster" from which that later and more familiar figure grew. By limiting the historical action in the drama, Racine achieves a tremendous concentration upon a single incident, which itself represents the central recurring conflict in Nero's life: whether or not to commit a crime.[19] In like manner, Rossellini captures Louis XIV at the precise moment the young monarch creates himself by actively assuming a political role on a stage of his own creation, Versailles. And in Rossellini's interpretation of the Sun King, one may also detect a subtle metaphor for the director himself. Louis and Rossellini share a strange aesthetic affinity, for social artifice and role playing lie at the heart of political power, just as cinematic artifice (foregrounded by Rossellini's frequent zooms and the special effects employing the Schüfftan process) constitutes the foundation of the cinema, even a supposedly "realist" cinema that aims at re-creating the historical past as accurately as possible.

Perhaps the most amazing aspect of *La prise de pouvoir par Louis XIV* is that Rossellini succeeds in producing his most convincing depiction of the "reality" of another historical period with a cinematic style that paradoxically celebrates the triumph of appearance over reality.

Notes

1. Rossellini and Realism

1. For all details concerning Rossellini's life, I follow the superb critical biography by Gianni Rondolino, *Roberto Rossellini* (Turin: UTET, 1989). The most comprehensive treatment of Rossellini in English, Peter Brunette's *Roberto Rossellini* (New York: Oxford University Press, 1987), contains a thorough discussion of each of Rossellini's films but has less biographical information than Rondolino's study. For critical bibliographies on Rossellini, see two useful books: Adriano Aprà, ed., *Rosselliniana: bibliografia internazionale, dossier "Paisà"* (Rome: Di Giacomo Editore, 1987); and Patrizio Rossi, *Roberto Rossellini: A Guide to References and Resources* (Boston: G. K. Hall, 1988), which covers publications through 1978. The most recent Italian publication on Rossellini's cinema, Fernaldo Di Giammatteo's *Roberto Rossellini* (Florence: La Nuova Italia, 1990), is especially important for the large number of fascinating photographs and Rossellini memorabilia that it includes.

2. As Rondolino (*Roberto Rossellini*, p. 359) notes, there is conflicting testimony over whether Rossellini ever possessed a membership card in the Fascist Party. It is clear that the film industry was less demanding of such outward manifestations of party loyalty (especially for a man intimate with the dictator's son) than it was for other professions; however, it is also equally true that it would have been extremely unusual for a man in Rossellini's position not to have possessed a party card.

3. Cited by Lino Micciché, "Il cadavere nell'armadio," in Riccardo Redi, ed., *Cinema italiano sotto il fascismo* (Venice: Marsilio Editori, 1979), p. 9. Unless otherwise indicated in this book, all translations from the Italian are mine. Redi's anthology collects the important papers delivered at the 1976 conference dedicated to fascist cinema that marked the beginning of a completely new critical perspective on this period. For discussions of cinema under fascism in English, see Adriano Aprà and Patrizia Pistagnesi, eds., *The Fabulous Thirties: Italian Cinema, 1929–1944* (Milan: Electa International, 1979); James Hay, *Italian Film Culture in Fascist Italy: The Passing of the Rex* (Bloomington: Indiana University Press, 1987); and Marcia Landy, *Fascism in Film: The Italian Commercial Cinema, 1931–1943* (Princeton: Princeton University Press, 1986). The most complete listing of the films produced during the fascist period may be found in the indispensable catalogue by

Francesco Savio, *Ma l'amore no: realismo, formalismo, propaganda e telefoni bianchi nel cinema italiano di regime (1930–1943)* (Milan: Sonzogno, 1975).

4. Micciché ("Il cadavere nell'armadio," in Redi, ed., *Cinema italiano*, pp. 11–13) cites figures on the number of extant prints viewable today.

5. For analyses of such newsreels, see Massimo Cardillo, *Il Duce in moviola: politica e divismo nei cinegiornali e documentari "Luce"* (Bari: Edizioni Dedalo, 1983); and Ernesto G. Laura, *L'immagine bugiarda: mass-media e spettacolo nella Repubblica di Salò (1943–1945)* (Rome: ANCCI, 1987).

6. For a discussion of the regime's attitudes, see Elaine Mancini, *Struggles of the Italian Film Industry during Fascism, 1930–1935* (Ann Arbor: University of Michigan Research Press, 1985); Sam Rohdie, "Capital and Realism in the Italian Cinema: An Examination of Film in the Fascist Period," *Screen* 24, no. 4–5 (1983), 37–46; and David Ellwood, "Italy: The Regime, the Nation, and the Film Industry: An Introduction," in K. R. M. Short, ed., *Film and Radio Propaganda in World War II* (Knoxville: University of Tennessee Press, 1983), pp. 220–29.

7. In "Emancipazione del cinema italiano," *Cinema* 1, no. 6 (1936), 213–15, Vittorio Mussolini explicitly calls for the transformation of the Italian cinema along the lines of the Hollywood model. Vittorio Mussolini visited Hollywood in 1937 and actually founded a production company with Hal Roach (R.A.M., Roach and Mussolini), which never really got off the ground (Rondolino, *Roberto Rossellini*, p. 35).

8. Leo Longanesi, "The Glass Eye," in Aprà and Pistagnesi, eds., *The Fabulous Thirties*, p. 50. Although Longanesi eventually turned away from the regime, as did so many left-wing Fascists who were disappointed with the conservative bent of Mussolini once he attained power, his initial support was nevertheless genuine, and he is even credited with having invented the infamous slogan *"Mussolini ha sempre ragione"* ("Mussolini is always right").

9. Zavattini's manifesto may be found in translation in David Overbey, ed., *Springtime in Italy: A Reader on Neo-Realism* (Hamden, Conn.: Archon Books, 1979), pp. 67–78.

10. For the best discussion of this phenomenon in English, to which this discussion is indebted, see Gianni Rondolino, "Italian Propaganda Films: 1940–1943," in Short, ed., *Film and Radio Propaganda in World War II*, pp. 230–44.

11. For detailed information on the director's career and his films, see Sergio G. Germani and Vittorio Martinelli, eds., *Il cinema di Augusto Genina* (Paisan di Prato: Edizioni Biblioteca dell'Immagine, 1989); a briefer discussion in English can be found in Landy, *Fascism in Film*, pp. 218–22.

12. For Antonioni's review and the complete credits of the film, see Savio, *Ma l'amore no*, pp. 29–30.

13. Cited from Rondolino, "Italian Propaganda Films," in Short, ed., *Film and Radio Propaganda in World War II*, p. 236; for the complete Italian text of the letter, see Luigi Freddi, *Il cinema* (Rome: L'Arnia, 1949), 1:207–11.

14. Cited by Rondolino in Short, ed., *Film and Radio Propaganda in World War II*, p. 237.

15. In the critical literature, *La nave bianca*, *Un pilota ritorna*, and *L'uomo dalla croce* are generally labeled the fascist trilogy, and *Roma città aperta*, *Paisà*, and *Germania anno zero* are termed the neorealist trilogy. It should be noted that these

distinctions are inventions of the critics and that Rossellini himself never intended to produce a trilogy, or a coherently conceived project in three parts, in either case.

16. For a sympathetic biography of Anna Magnani, see Patrizia Carrano's *La Magnani: il romanzo di una vita* (Milan: Rizzoli, 1986).

17. For a discussion of this landmark decision, see Ellen Draper, " 'Controversy Has Probably Destroyed Forever the Context': *The Miracle* and Movie Censorship in America in the Fifties," *The Velvet Light Trap* 25 (1990), 69–79. The case (*Burstyn v. Wilson*) reversed a 1915 ruling.

18. Roberto Rossellini, "Ten Years of Cinema," in Overbey, ed., *Springtime in Italy*, p. 102.

19. Félix Morlion, "The Philosophical Basis of Neo-Realism," in Overbey, ed., *Springtime in Italy*, p. 122.

20. Ingrid Bergman, with Alan Burgess, *My Story* (New York: Delacorte, 1980), pp. 4–5.

21. Cited by Rondolino, *Roberto Rossellini*, p. 157.

22. Letter cited by Rondolino in *Roberto Rossellini*, p. 159.

23. Brunette, *Roberto Rossellini*, p. 111.

24. For the text of the complete interview, see Roberto Rossellini, *Il mio metodo*, ed. Adriano Aprà (Venice: Marsilio Editori, 1987), pp. 159–68.

25. For a collection of some of the articles devoted to Rossellini by this group, see Jim Hiller, ed., *Cahiers du Cinéma—The 1950s: Neo-Realism, Hollywood, New Wave* (Cambridge: Harvard University Press, 1985).

26. See Brunette, *Roberto Rossellini*, pp. 222–23, for a discussion of the zoom technique.

27. Although the last of these eleven works, *Anno uno* and *Il Messia,* were intended for theatrical release and have a wide-screen format, their basic style follows that of the television films.

28. For the texts of these discussions, see Rossellini, *Il mio metodo*, pp. 265–301.

29. For a discussion of Rossellini in Houston, see *Roberto Rossellini*, the catalogue for a 1987 retrospective entitled "Rossellini in Texas" (Rome: Ente Autonomo di Gestione per il Cinema, 1987), which contains a great deal of information on Rossellini's Texas sojourn.

30. Federico Fellini, "My Experiences as a Director," in Peter Bondanella, ed., *Federico Fellini: Essays in Criticism* (New York: Oxford University Press, 1978), pp. 3, 4.

2. L'uomo dalla croce

1. As is true of most war films in every country, Rossellini did employ a military consultant, Lieutenant Colonel D. U. Leonardi, on *L'uomo dalla croce*.

2. Cited in Roberto Rossellini, *Il mio metodo*, pp. 43–44; and in Rondolino, *Roberto Rossellini*, p. 22.

3. After Mussolini's downfall and the end of the war, it became fashionable for many leftist critics to deny that Italian fascism had ever possessed any political ideology. The most persuasive reply to this point of view can be found in three studies by A. James Gregor: *The Ideology of Fascism: The Rationale of Totalitarianism* (New York: Free Press, 1969); *Interpretations of Fascism* (Morristown, N.J.:

General Learning Press, 1974); and *Young Mussolini and the Intellectual Origins of Fascism* (Berkeley and Los Angeles: University of California Press, 1979). For an English anthology of representative fascist political writings, see Adrian Lyttelton, ed., *Italian Fascisms: From Pareto to Gentile* (London: Jonathan Cape, 1973).

4. Freddi, *Il cinema*, 2:419.

5. See, for example, the discussions of the fascist trilogy in Brunette, *Roberto Rossellini*, pp. 11–32; and Rondolino, *Roberto Rossellini*, pp. 48–63.

6. Rossellini, *Il mio metodo*, p. 88. The existing English translation of this interview (see Roberto Rossellini, "A Discussion of Neo-Realism: Rossellini Interviewed by Mario Verdone," *Screen* 14, no. 4 [1973–74], 69–77) is defective precisely in this specific passage, since it renders *coralità* as "human warmth" and completely distorts Rossellini's emphasis upon the group acting in unison, like a chorus, where no individual voices can be distinguished.

7. José Luis Guarner, *Roberto Rossellini*, trans. Elisabeth Cameron (New York: Praeger, 1970), p. 11.

8. Brunette (*Roberto Rossellini*, p. 31) believes the character to be an Italian turncoat.

9. In the absence of a printed script, I translate from the available American videocassette.

10. See Giuseppe De Santis, *Verso il neorealismo: un critico cinematografico degli anni quaranta*, ed. Callisto Cosulich (Rome: Bulzoni Editore, 1982), pp. 210–13, for the complete text of De Santis's review, which originally appeared in *Cinema* 168 (25 June 1943).

11. See Guarner, *Roberto Rossellini*, p. 11; and Brunette, *Roberto Rossellini*, pp. 27–29.

3. *Roma città aperta*

1. Fellini's account of this encounter with Geiger is found in Federico Fellini, *Fare un film* (Turin: Einaudi, 1976), pp. 73–74; it is only fair to record that Rod Geiger denied this version of Fellini's account in a personal telephone conversation (31 March 1990).

2. See, for example, Brunette, *Roberto Rossellini*, pp. 59–60; and Robert Burgoyne, "The Imaginary and the Neo-Real," *Enclitic* 3, no. 1 (1979), 16–34.

3. Rondolino (*Roberto Rossellini*, p. 81) gives these figures.

4. André Bazin, always the most sensitive critic of the period, emphasized the high quality of the acting in *Roma città aperta* and noted that it was not so much the replacement of professionals by nonprofessionals but, instead, the casting against conventional expectations that marked Rossellini's originality (*What Is Cinema? Volume II*, trans. Hugh Gray [Berkeley and Los Angeles: University of California Press, 1971], pp. 22, 23–24).

5. Brunette, *Roberto Rossellini*, p. 45. There are some important exceptions to this practice, however, that will be discussed.

6. Roberto Rossellini, *The War Trilogy*, ed. Stefano Roncoroni (New York: Grossman, 1973), p. 154.

7. See Millicent Marcus, *Italian Film in the Light of Neorealism*, (Princeton: Princeton University Press, 1986), pp. 44–46, for a good discussion of the film's humor.

8. For a very different interpretation of this sequence – in many instances arbitrary, forced, and even inaccurate, yet containing a number of heuristic ideas – see Burgoyne, "The Imaginary and the Neo-Real."

9. Rossellini, *The War Trilogy*, p. 152.

10. Martin Walsh, "Re-evaluating Rossellini," in Dan Ranvaud, ed., *Roberto Rossellini*, British Film Institute Dossier no. 8 (London, 1981), p. 52 (originally published in *Jump Cut* 15 [1977], 13–15).

11. Perhaps the purest form of this kind of thinking may be found in Robert P. Kolker, *The Altering Eye: Contemporary International Cinema* (New York: Oxford University Press, 1983), who faults Rossellini and the neorealists in general for failing to adopt Brechtian techniques and for relying on melodramatic means to manipulate an audience's emotions.

4. Paisà

1. For an Italian script of *Paisà*, as well as a collection of interviews on the film and an extensive Rossellini bibliography, see Aprà, ed., *Rosselliniana;* the English version of the script can be examined in Rossellini, *The War Trilogy.*

2. Bazin, *What Is Cinema?*, p. 34.

3. Bazin, *What Is Cinema?*, p. 37.

4. Brunette, *Roberto Rossellini*, p. 62.

5. Sergio Amidei notes this and also states that Rossellini chose the Amalfi coast location because it was near his then-unnamed mistress's home (in Aprà, ed., *Rosselliniana*, p. 108).

6. Massimo Mida, the assistant director on the film, notes this (in Aprà, ed., *Rosselliniana*, p. 137).

7. Franca Faldini and Goffredo Fofi, eds., *L'avventurosa storia del cinema italiano raccontata dai suoi protagonisti, 1935–1959* (Milan: Feltrinelli, 1979), p. 108.

8. Massimo Mida, in Aprà, ed., *Rosselliniana*, p. 139.

9. See Fellini's comments in Faldini and Fofi, eds., *L'avventurosa storia del cinema italiano, 1935–1959*, p. 108.

10. See Rod Geiger's remarks in Aprà, ed., *Rosselliniana*, pp. 131–32.

11. Massimo Mida, in Aprà, ed., *Rosselliniana*, p. 109.

12. Stefano Masi and Enrico Lancia, *I film di Roberto Rossellini* (Rome: Gremese Editore, 1987), p. 29.

13. Rossellini, *The War Trilogy*, p. 177.

14. Rossellini, *The War Trilogy*, p. 180.

15. Rossellini, *The War Trilogy*, pp. 183, 185, lists these shots (numbered 93 and 94 in the episode, which contains 161 shots) as lasting for 1 minute 34 seconds and 4 minutes 12 seconds.

16. Rossellini, *The War Trilogy*, pp. 184–85.

17. Rossellini, *The War Trilogy*, p. 201.

18. Rossellini, *The War Trilogy*, p. 216.

19. Rossellini, *The War Trilogy*, pp. 238–39.

20. For a more extensive analysis of Fellini's work as a scriptwriter for Rossellini and other neorealist directors, see my *The Cinema of Federico Fellini* (Princeton: Princeton University Press, 1992).

21. A number of critics have noted Rossellini's obvious anti-British bias in *Paisà*, a sentiment that is also expressed in the final, Po Valley sequence when General Alexander's orders to the partisans to cease hostilities provoke a sarcastic comment from Dale, the American liaison officer: "These people aren't fighting for the British Empire. They're fighting for their lives" (Rossellini, *The War Trilogy*, p. 322).

22. For a description of this early version, see Aprà, ed., *Rosselliniana*, p. 129.

23. Rossellini, *The War Trilogy*, pp. 315–16. For Boccaccio's story, placed near the beginning of *The Decameron* (Day I, Story 3) to assert the author's own religious tolerance, see Giovanni Boccaccio, *The Decameron*, trans. Mark Musa and Peter Bondanella (New York: New American Library, 1982), pp. 36–38. If Fellini and Rossellini were influenced by Boccaccio, as I believe to be the case, they transformed the three rings representing the three great monotheistic religions (Christianity, Judaism, Islam) into three chaplains of three different faiths.

24. Rossellini, *The War Trilogy*, p. 348.

25. Bazin, *What Is Cinema?*, p. 34. Bazin's definition is based on only a small part of the Po Valley sequence. For an application of Bazin's theories to the first episode, situated in Sicily, see Michael Sinclair, "Ellipsis in Rossellini's *Paisà*: The Privileging of the Invisible," *Spectator* 9, no. 1 (1988), 38–55.

5. La macchina ammazzacattivi

1. Bazin, *What Is Cinema?*, p. 26.

2. Roy Armes, *Patterns of Realism: A Study of Italian Neo-Realism* (Cranbury, N.J.: A. S. Barnes, 1971), p. 188. Armes provides an excellent discussion of the artistic implications of neorealism and a number of cogent reasons for the necessity of the transition beyond neorealism, to which my discussion here is indebted.

3. The most accessible collection of the essays on Rossellini and neorealism by the French intellectuals of the *Cahiers* group (Bazin, Amédée Ayfre, Jacques Rivette, Eric Rohmer, François Truffaut, Fereydoun Hoveyda) can be found in Hiller, ed., *Cahiers du Cinéma*.

4. Armes, *Patterns of Realism*, p. 192.

5. The entire polemical struggle boiled over at the 1954 Venice Biennale Film Festival, where Fellini's *La strada* and Visconti's *Senso* were championed, respectively, by critics such as Bazin, who approved of the new directions beyond neorealism, and by Italian Marxists, led by Guido Aristarco and the group around the Marxist film journal *Cinema Nuovo*, who attacked Fellini and other like-minded directors, such as Rossellini, whose turn toward a more introspective cinema included elements of Christian morality. For a collection of the polemical articles concerned with what has been termed the "crisis" of neorealism, see Federico Fellini, *"La Strada": Federico Fellini, Director*, ed. Peter Bondanella and Manuela Gieri (New Brunswick, N.J.: Rutgers University Press, 1987), pp. 197–220.

6. Fellini, *"La Strada,"* p. 207.

7. Fellini, *"La Strada,"* p. 217.

8. Cited by Pierre Leprohon in *Michelangelo Antonioni: An Introduction*, trans. Scott Sullivan (New York: Simon and Schuster, 1963), pp. 89–90.

9. Vittorio De Sica, *Miracle in Milan* (Baltimore: Penguin, 1969), p. 13.

10. Masi and Lancia, *I film di Roberto Rossellini,* pp. 40–41, provides the most specific information available on the making of this film.

11. Rossellini, "Rossellini si defende," in Rossellini, *Il mio metodo,* p. 65.

12. An English translation, marred by the serious error of rendering *coralità* as "human warmth" rather than "choral quality," may be found in Rossellini, "A Discussion of Neo-Realism;" for the original, see Rossellini, "Colloquio sul neo-realismo a cura di Mario Verdone," in Rossellini, *Il mio metodo,* pp. 84–94.

13. Rossellini, *Il mio metodo,* p. 93.

14. Hiller, ed., *Cahiers du Cinéma,* p. 209.

15. In the absence of a published script in either Italian or English, I cite the English subtitles from the print distributed in the United States.

16. In *Roberto Rossellini: i suoi film (1936–1972) e la filmografia completa* (Rome: Edizioni Samonà e Savelli, 1972), p. 85, Marxist critic Pio Baldelli attacks the film for presenting such a classless universe of greedy individuals. A portrayal of the poor as equal to the rich in their selfishness can also be found in Vittorio De Sica's *Miracolo a Milano,* released during the same year as *La macchina ammazzacattivi* with probably the same polemical intent. More recently, Ettore Scola has depicted the poor in a contemporary shantytown in even more unfavorable terms in *Brutti, sporchi, e cattivi (Dirty, Mean, and Nasty,* 1976), which is itself an homage to his cinematic model De Sica and the earlier *Miracolo a Milano.* Rossellini, De Sica, and Scola all seem to be deflating the popular Marxist notion that members of the Italian working class, solely by virtue of their class affiliation, possess some degree of moral superiority over others.

17. Brunette (*Roberto Rossellini,* p. 104), also makes this point.

6. Viaggio in Italia

1. Cited in Masi and Lancia, *I film di Roberto Rossellini,* p. 63 (Marino Onorati writing in *Film d'Oggi*).

2. Cited by Masi and Lancia, *Il film di Roberto Rossellini,* p. 64 (Ezio Colombo writing in *Festival*).

3. The listing is reprinted in Hiller, ed., *Cahiers du Cinéma,* pp. 287–88. A ranking in 1955 that covered only that year put Rossellini's film at the top of the list.

4. Jacques Rivette, "Letter on Rossellini," in Hiller, ed., *Cahiers du Cinéma,* pp. 192, 202 (the original appeared in the April 1955 issue).

5. Eric Rohmer, "The Land of Miracles," in Hiller, ed., *Cahiers du Cinéma,* p. 205 (the original appeared in the May 1955 issue written under the author's real name, Maurice Schérer).

6. André Bazin, "In Defense of Rossellini," in Bazin, *What is Cinema?,* p. 101 (the original appeared in the August 1955 issue of *Cinema Nuovo*).

7. Roberto Rossellini, "Rossellini on Rossellini," *Screen* 14, no. 4 (1973–74), 80 (the original French interview appeared in *La Table Ronde* in May 1960).

8. Guarner, *Roberto Rossellini,* p. 58; Guarner's suggestion that the film is an essay reflects Rivette's original suggestion (Hiller, ed., *Cahiers du Cinéma,* p. 199).

9. Eric Rohmer and François Truffaut, "Interview with Roberto Rossellini," in Hiller, ed., *Cahiers du Cinéma,* p. 212.

10. George Sanders, *Memoirs of a Professional Cad* (New York: Putnam's, 1960), p. 119.

11. Sanders, *Memoirs of a Professional Cad*, p. 122.

12. Ingrid Bergman, with Alan Burgess, *My Story*, p. 307.

13. Jacques Rivette, "Letter on Rossellini," in Hiller, ed., *Cahiers du Cinéma*, p. 200.

14. Kolker (*The Altering Eye*, p. 133) makes this point very forcefully.

15. Robin Wood, "Rossellini," *Film Comment* 10, no. 4 (1974), 9.

16. Roberto Rossellini, "Ten Years of Cinema," in Overbey, ed., *Springtime in Italy*, p. 98.

17. Eric Rohmer and François Truffaut, "Interviews with Roberto Rossellini," in Hiller, ed. *Cahiers du Cinéma*, p. 210.

18. Rohmer and Truffaut, "Interviews with Roberto Rossellini," in Hiller, ed., *Cahiers du Cinéma*, pp. 212–13.

19. Brunette (*Roberto Rossellini*, p. 165) makes this point very well; the same argument is contained in his essay "Visual Motifs in Rossellini's *Voyage to Italy*," in Peter Lehman, ed., *Close Viewings: An Anthology of New Film Criticism* (Tallahassee: Florida State University Press, 1990), pp. 49–50.

20. In the absence of a script in either Italian or English, I am citing from the English dialogue in the original film. *Viaggio in Italia* was originally shot in synchronized sound and in English. A great deal of the important dialogue in this scene may also be found in Brunette, *Roberto Rossellini*, pp. 168–69.

21. For the original interview, see Roberto Rossellini, "Film vecchi e nuovi orizzonti," in Rossellini, *Il mio metodo*, pp. 333–52. An English translation may be consulted in "An Interview with Roberto Rossellini by Adriano Aprà and Maurizio Ponzi," *Screen* 14, no. 4 (1973–74), 112–26, but it should be compared with the original Italian for accuracy, since it is deficient precisely in the section concerning Rossellini's comments about the ending of *Viaggio in Italia*.

22. My translation from Rossellini, *Il mio metodo*, p. 334; for the *Screen* version, which ignores the important word *"Certo,"* see p. 112 of "An interview with Roberto Rossellini by Adriano Aprà and Maurizio Ponzi." Peter Brunette seems to misconstrue Rossellini's position in this interview as a result of his reliance upon the English version of the Italian original. He bases his own interpretation of the scene upon the erroneous claim that "Rossellini does not explicitly agree that it is 'a false happy ending' " (*Roberto Rossellini*, p. 169).

23. See Kolker, *The Altering Eye*, pp. 130–31, 134, for a discussion of this problem.

7. Il generale Della Rovere

1. Roberto Rossellini, "Panoramica sulla storia," in Rossellini, *Il mio metodo*, p. 381.

2. Brunette (*Roberto Rossellini*, p. 212) provides these revealing figures on costs and gross income for the film.

3. In the absence of a published script, I quote from the print of the film available in the United States. For a version of the short story by Montanelli that is an elaboration of the script and published subsequent to the film's release, see Indro Montanelli, *Il generale Della Rovere* (Milan: Rizzoli, 1959).

4. Rossellini discusses this lack of warm, personal links to the new generation of

Italian filmmakers, in contrast to his paternal relationship to artists such as Truffaut, in "Verso la televisione, e oltre," in Rossellini, *Il mio metodo,* p. 368.

5. Guarner, *Roberto Rossellini,* p. 78.

6. Brunette, *Roberto Rossellini,* p. 211; Brunette, however, recognizes many of the elements indicating Rossellini's ambivalent notion of cinematic realism that I emphasize in this chapter.

7. For important studies of De Sica as actor, see Francesco Bolzoni, *Quando De Sica Era Mister Brown* (Turin: ERI, 1984); and especially Vincenzo Mollica, ed. *Le canzoni di Vittorio De Sica* (Montepulciano: Editori del Grifo, 1990). The latter work, a booklet accompanying a collection of De Sica's most famous songs, contains many examples from popular gossip and film reviews of the 1930s that give the most accurate reflection of De Sica's persona in the Italian cinema of the period.

8. In the absence of a published script, I translate from the original Italian dialogue on the print released in the United States.

9. This commonly overlooked detail is noted by Masi and Lancia, *I film di Roberto Rossellini,* p. 82.

10. This modified zoom lens that Rossellini personally devised (known as a *"carello ottico"* in Italian and a *"travelling optique"* in French) will be discussed in Chapter 8.

11. Wood, "Rossellini," p. 8.

12. Leo Braudy, "From *Open City* to *General Della Rovere*," in Leo Braudy and Morris Dickstein, eds., *Great Film Directors: A Critical Anthology* (New York: Oxford University Press, 1978), p. 673.

8. La prise de pouvoir par Louis XIV

1. Rossellini, "I mezzi audiovisivi e l'uomo della civiltà scientifica e industriale," in Rossellini, *Il mio metodo,* pp. 252–64. Rossellini's writings about television and mass culture may be found collected in this volume and in Sergio Trasatti, *Rossellini e la televisione* (Rome: La Rassegna Editrice, 1978).

2. See "Intervista con i *Cahiers du Cinéma* a cura di Jean Domarchi e Fereydoun Hoveyda (3)," in Rossellini, *Il mio metodo,* p. 269.

3. See Rossellini, "Intervista con i *Cahiers du Cinéma* a cura di Fereydoun Hoveyda e Eric Rohmer (4)," in Rossellini, *Il mio metodo,* pp. 288–301.

4. See Rossellini, "Difendere la speranza che è dentro di noi," in Rossellini, *Il mio metodo,* pp. 328–32.

5. For the Italian original, see Rossellini, "Film vecchi e nuovi orizzonti," in Rossellini, *Il mio metodo,* pp. 337, 338; for the English translation from which I cite, see "An Interview with Roberto Rossellini by Adriano Aprà and Maurizio Ponzi," *Screen* 14, no. 4 (1973–74), 114, 115.

6. For the Italian original, see Rossellini, "Manifesto," in Rossellini, *Il mio metodo,* pp. 353–54; I cite the English translation in Rossellini, "Rossellini's Manifesto," *Screen* 14, no. 4 (1973–74), 110.

7. Rossellini, "Intervista con i *Cahiers du Cinéma* (5)," in Rossellini, *Il mio metodo,* p. 365.

8. Rossellini, "Contro le teorie estetiche a cura di Tag Gallagher e John Hughes,"

in Rossellini, *Il mio metodo*, pp. 443–61; an English version appeared in *Changes* 87 (1974).

9. For examples of critical discussions of Rossellini that rely upon Brecht's theories, see John Hughes, "Recent Rossellini," *Film Comment* 10, no. 4 (1974), 16–21; James Roy MacBean, *Film and Revolution* (Bloomington: Indiana University Press, 1975), pp. 209–29 ("Rossellini's Materialist Mise-en-Scène of *La prise de pouvoir par Louis XIV*"); Walsh, "Re-evaluating Rossellini." Peter Brunette ("Just How Brechtian Is Rossellini?" *Film Criticism* 3, no. 2 [1979], 30–42) presents a sensible corrective to the critical excesses of such analogies (a point of view also incorporated into his book, *Roberto Rossellini*). For a more charitable view of Brecht and Godard in relationship to contemporary film, see Kolker, *The Altering Eye*.

10. For a discussion of the details of Rossellini's innovations with his Pancinor zoom lens, see Di Giammatteo, *Roberto Rossellini*, p. 159.

11. For a discussion of the Schüfftan process, see Di Giammatteo, *Roberto Rossellini*, pp. 159–70, which includes several excellent photographs from work on the set demonstrating Rossellini's use of the process; James Monaco, *How to Read a Film: The Art, Technology, Language, History, and Theory of Film and Media* (New York: Oxford University Press, 1977); and John Brosnian, *Movie Magic: The Story of Special Effects in the Cinema* (New York: New American Library, 1976).

12. See Peter Bondanella, *The Eternal City: Roman Images in the Modern World* (Chapel Hill: University of North Carolina Press, 1987), pp. 215, 224–27, for a discussion of *Cleopatra* and *The Fall of the Roman Empire*.

13. For a discussion of this historical genre, see Peter Bondanella, *Italian Cinema: From Neorealism to the Present*, 2d rev. ed. (New York: Continuum, 1990), pp. 159; and Derek Elley, *The Epic Film: Myth and History* (London: Routledge and Kegan Paul, 1984).

14. How far such a desire to see Rossellini as a Marxist may take some critics can be seen in the political interpretation of the opening sequence of the film. Many of the articles written by U.S. and English critics declare that the figures at the bank of a river washing clothes and talking are peasants because some of them are criticizing the monarchy. This is supposedly the only representation of the Marxist proletariat in Rossellini's film, and therefore, for a good Marxist critic, it cannot be ignored. But the clothing of these characters cannot possibly be that of peasants; indeed their dialogue, speaking of sons as wine merchants and daughters working at the court, reveals that they belong to quite a different economic class, the lower middle class or the merchant class, which will eventually bring about the French Revolution, overturning the very monarchy Louis XIV devoted his life to protecting.

15. In the absence of a printed script, I cite from the subtitles of the print distributed in the United States.

16. MacBean, *Film and Revolution*, p. 215.

17. Niccolò Machiavelli, *The Prince*, ed. Peter Bondanella (Oxford: Oxford University Press, 1984), p. 60; for a complete treatment of the theme of reality and appearance in Machiavelli's works, see Wayne Rebhorn, *Lions and Foxes: Machiavelli's Confidence Men* (Ithaca: Cornell University Press, 1988).

18. Guarner, *Roberto Rossellini*, p. 116.

19. For a discussion of the concentrated narrative form of French classical theater,

see Will G. Moore, *French Classical Literature: An Essay* (Oxford: Oxford University Press, 1961). Bondanella (*The Eternal City: Roman Images in the Modern World,* pp. 101–14) analyzes this kind of drama in French theater and operatic melodrama in Italy, both of which were probably influential in Rossellini's creation of the storyline of *La prise de pouvoir par Louis XIV.*

Chronology

1906 Rossellini is born in Rome on 8 May; Giosuè Carducci wins the Nobel Prize for Literature

1909 Filippo Marinetti publishes the Futurist Manifesto in Paris

1915 Griffith's *Birth of a Nation* is released

1921 The Italian Communist Party is founded; Luigi Pirandello's *Sei personaggi in cerca d'autore* is first performed

1922 Mussolini's March on Rome on 27–28 October begins the fascist era; publication of Joyce's *Ulysses* and Eliot's *The Waste Land*

1926 Grazia Deledda wins the Nobel Prize for Literature (the first Italian woman to receive the prize)

1929 Mussolini and the Catholic church sign the Lateran Pact

1934 Hitler and Mussolini meet in Venice; Luigi Pirandello wins the Nobel Prize for Literature

1935 Italy invades Ethiopia in October

1936 Rossellini begins making short films; Mussolini proclaims the Empire in May 1936 after the conquest of Ethiopia; on 26 September Rossellini marries Marcella De Marchis

1937 Rossellini's first son, Romano, is born on 3 July

1938 Enrico Fermi wins the Nobel Prize for Physics; the Munich Peace Conference is held in September; Rossellini works on *Luciano Serra, pilota*

1939 Germany invades Poland and World War II begins

1940 Italy joins the war on the side of Nazi Germany and invades France on 10 June

1941 Rossellini makes *La nave bianca;* Mussolini sends the Italian Expeditionary Force to Russia in June

1942 Rossellini makes *Un pilota ritorna*

1943 Rossellini makes *L'uomo dalla croce;* the Allies invade Sicily on 10 June; on 24–25 July, the Fascist Grand Council abandons Mussolini, and Marshal Pietro Badoglio is named prime minister; Mussolini is arrested on 25 July; on 8 September, Italy signs an armistice with the Allies and declares war on Germany but the king and Badoglio are forced to flee Rome; on

	12–13 September, Mussolini is rescued by the Germans at Gran Sasso and is taken north to head the Republic of Salò; on 1 October, Naples is liberated
1944	Rome is liberated in June
1945	Rossellini makes *Roma città aperta;* on 28 April, Mussolini is executed by partisans
1946	Rossellini makes *Paisà;* Romano Rossellini dies on 14 August in Barcelona; Erich Auerbach writes *Mimesis;* Rossellini's affair with Anna Magnani begins
1947	*Germania anno zero* is shot; in May the Socialists and the Communists are ejected from the coalition government in Italy's parliament
1948	On 1 January, Italy proclaims a republic and abolishes the monarchy; on 18 April, the Christian Democrats win victory at the first postwar elections; Rossellini makes *L'amore* and begins *La macchina ammazzacattivi*
1949	Italy joins NATO; Rossellini makes *Stromboli* and begins his affair with Ingrid Bergman
1950	Rossellini makes *Francesco, giullare di Dio*
1951	Antonio Gramsci's *Prison Notebooks* appear posthumously
1952	Rossellini makes *Europa '51;* Benedetto Croce dies
1953	Rossellini's *Viaggio in Italia* and Federico Fellini's *I vitelloni* appear; Joseph Stalin dies
1954	Rossellini's *La paura* appears; at the Venice Biennale, the screenings of Fellini's *La strada* and Luchino Visconti's *Senso* provoke heated controversies over the proper direction of Italian neorealism; in Paris, from 1954 to 1956, Rossellini meets the critics and future directors associated with the journal *Cahiers du Cinéma*
1956	Rossellini departs for India, ending his affair with Ingrid Bergman and beginning an affair with Sonali Senroy
1957	The European Common Market is formed; the Soviet Union launches *Sputnik I*
1958	Giuseppe Tomasi di Lampedusa's *The Leopard* becomes a worldwide bestseller; Rossellini completes his documentary on India
1959	Rossellini's *Il generale Della Rovere* wins the Golden Lion Award at the Venice Biennale; Federico Fellini's *La dolce vita* establishes box-office records for a European film; Salvatore Quasimodo wins the Nobel Prize for Literature
1960	Rossellini completes *Era notte a Roma;* Pier Paolo Pasolini's *Accattone* and Michelangelo Antonioni's *La notte* appear
1963	Fellini's *8 1/2* appears; Giorgio Strehler produces Bertolt Brecht's *Galileo* in Milan; Jean-Luc Godard's *Les carabiniers* is made from Rossellini's subject
1964	Rossellini abandons the traditional cinema and turns to television films with *L'età del ferro;* Pasolini's *Il vangelo secondo Matteo* and Sergio Leone's *Un pugno di dollari* (the first successful "spaghetti western") are released
1966	Rossellini's television masterpiece, *La prise de pouvoir par Louis XIV,* is made; the Cultural Revolution begins in China

1967	Antonioni's *Blow Up* appears
1969	Rossellini is named to head the Centro sperimentale di cinematografia; Americans land on the moon
1970	Rossellini's *Socrate* is made for television
1971	Rossellini films an interview with Salvador Allende in Chile and makes a documentary at Rice University in the United States
1972	*Blaise Pascal, Agostino d'Ippona,* and *L'età di Cosimo de' Medici* are completed for Italian television; Bernardo Bertolucci's *Last Tango in Paris* is a worldwide success; Henry Moore's Florence exhibit takes place
1973	Fellini wins his fifth Oscar for Best Foreign Film with *Amarcord;* Rossellini makes *Cartesio* for television
1974	Rossellini makes a brief but unsuccessful return to commercial cinema with *Anno uno;* Richard Nixon resigns as president of the United States
1975	Pier Paolo Pasolini is murdered; Eugenio Montale wins the Nobel Prize for Literature; Rossellini makes *Il Messia*
1976	Umberto Eco publishes *A Theory of Semiotics*
1977	Rossellini makes his last two documentary films and presides over the jury at the Cannes Film Festival; he dies on 3 June and is buried on 6 June in Rome

Filmography

Dafne (Daphne). 1936

Prélude à l'après-midi d'un faune (Prelude to the Afternoon of a Faun). 1936

Fantasia sottomarina (A Fantasy of the Deep). 1939
Subject: Roberto Rossellini
Screenplay: Roberto Rossellini
Photography: Rodolfo Lombardi
Editing: Roberto Rossellini
Music: Edoardo Micucci
Producer: Incom/Esperia Films
Length: About 10 minutes

Il tacchino prepotente (The Overbearing Turkey). 1939
Subject: Roberto Rossellini
Screenplay: Roberto Rossellini
Photography: Mario Bava
Editing: Roberto Rossellini

In compiling this filmography, I have relied primarily upon three books: Peter Brunette's *Roberto Rossellini* (whose translations of English titles I generally follow); Masi and Lancia's *I film di Roberto Rossellini*, the filmography of which contains information on the length of films and their first television transmission that Brunette's filmography does not contain; and Rondolino's *Roberto Rossellini,* which is the most detailed source for premiers and awards. When an entry is omitted from the filmography, the information was unavailable or not applicable to the film in question.

La vispa Teresa (Lively Teresa). 1939
Subject: Roberto Rossellini
Screenplay: Roberto Rossellini
Photography: Mario Bava
Editing: Roberto Rossellini

Il ruscello di Ripasottile (The Brook of Ripasottile). 1941
Subject: Roberto Rossellini
Screenplay: Roberto Rossellini
Photography: Rodolfo Lombardi
Editing: Roberto Rossellini
Music: Umberto Mancini
Producer: Franco Riganti for Excelsior-Saci

La nava bianca (The White Ship). 1941
Subject: Francesco De Robertis
Screenplay: Francesco De Robertis, Roberto Rossellini
Photography: Giuseppe Caracciolo
Editing: Eraldo Da Roma
Music: Renzo Rossellini
Sound: Piero Cavazzuti
Set design: Amleto Bonetti
Producer: Scalera Film and Centro cinematografico del Ministero della marina
Cast: Nonprofessional actors
Length: 77 minutes
First screening or transmission (if intended for television): Milan, 15 October 1941
Awards: Cup of the National Fascist Party (Venice Biennale, 1941)

Un pilota ritorna (A Pilot Returns). 1942
Subject: Tito Silvio Mursino (Vittorio Mussolini)
Screenplay: Michelangelo Antonioni, Rosario Leone, Margherita Maglione, Massimo Mida, Roberto Rossellini
Photography: Vincenzo Seratrice
Editing: Eraldo Da Roma
Music: Renzo Rossellini
Sound: Franco Robecchi
Set design: Virgilio Marchi, Franco Bartoli
Producer: Anonima Cinematografica Italiana

Military advisers: Major Filippo Masoero, Captain Aldo Moggi
Cast: Massimo Girotti (Lieutenant Gino Rossati), Michela Belmonte (Anna), Gaetano Masier (Lieutenant Trisotti), and officers and men of the Italian air force
Length: 87 minutes
First screening or transmission (if intended for television): Rome, 9 April 1942
Awards: National Cinematography Prize for the Best War or Political Film (Italy, 1942).

L'uomo dalla croce *(The Man with a Cross).* 1943

Subject: Asvero Gravelli
Screenplay: Asvero Gravelli, Roberto Rossellini, Alberto Consiglio, G. D'Alicandro
Photography: Guglielmo Lombardi, Aurelio Attili
Music: Renzo Rossellini
Set design: Gastone Medin
Producer: Continentalcine
Military adviser: Lieutenant Colonel D. U. Leonardi
Cast: Alberto Tavazzi (the chaplain), Roswita Schmidt (Irina), Attilo Dottesio (Fyodor), Aldo Capacci (Sergei), Doris Hild, Franco Castellani, Ruggero Isnenghi, Antonio Marietti, Piero Pastore, Marcello Tanzi, Zoia Weneda
Length: 88 minutes
First screening or transmission (if intended for television): Milan, 16 June 1943

Desiderio *(Desire).* 1943–46 [Completed in 1946 by Marcello Pagliero]

Subject: Anna Benvenuti
Screenplay: Rosario Leone, Roberto Rossellini, Diego Calcagno, Giuseppe De Santis; with additional material added by Marcello Pagliero and Guglielmo Santangelo to the footage shot by Pagliero in 1946
Assistant director: Giuseppe De Santis (for Rossellini)
Photography: Rodolfo Lombardi (for Rossellini), Ugo Lombardi (for Pagliero)
Music: Renzo Rossellini
Producer: Sovrania Film/Società Anomina Film Italiani Roma
Cast: Elli Parvo (Paola Previtali), Massimo Girotti (Nando Selvini), Carlo Ninchi (Giovanni Mirelli), Roswita Schmidt (Anna Previtali Selvini), and others

Length: 102 minutes (85 minutes after cuts by censor)
First screening or transmission (if intended for television): Rome, 9 September 1946

Roma città aperta *(Open City).* 1945
Subject: Sergio Amidei, Alberto Consiglio (not credited)
Screenplay: Sergio Amidei, Federico Fellini, Roberto Rossellini, Alberto Consiglio (not credited)
Assistant directors: Sergio Amidei, Federico Fellini, Mario Chiari (not credited)
Photography: Ubaldo Arata
Cameramen: Vincenzo Seratrice, assisted by Carlo Carlini, Carlo Di Palma, Gianni Di Venanzo
Editing: Eraldo Da Roma
Music: Renzo Rossellini
Sound: Raffaele Del Monte
Set design: Renato Megna, Mario Chiari (not credited)
Producer: Excelsa Film; Contessa Carla Politi and Aldo Venturini (not credited)
Cast: Aldo Fabrizi (Don Pietro), Anna Magnani (Pina), Marcello Pagliero (Giorgio Manfredi, alias Luigi Ferraris), Francesco Grandjacquet (Francesco), Harry Feist (Major Bergmann), Maria Michi (Marina), Giovanna Galletti (Ingrid), Carla Rovera (Lauretta, Pina's sister), Joop Van Hulzsen (Hartmann), Alberto Tavizzi (priest at execution), Carlo Sindici (the *questore*), Vito Annichiarico (Marcello, Pina's son), Nando Bruno (Agostino, the sacristan), Edoardo Passarelli (the policeman), Aklos Tolnay (the Austrian deserter)
Length: 100 minutes
First screening or transmission (if intended for television): Rome, 24 September 1945
Awards: Grand Prize at Cannes Film Festival (1946); New York Film Critics Award for Best Foreign Film (1946)

Paisà *(Paisan).* 1946
Subject: Sergio Amidei, with the collaboration of Federico Fellini, Alfred Hayes, Klaus Mann, Marcello Pagliero, Roberto Rossellini
Screenplay: Sergio Amidei, Federico Fellini, Roberto Rossellini, Vasco Pratolini (for the Florence episode)
Assistant directors: Federico Fellini, Massimo Mida, E. Handamir, Annalena Limentani, Renzo Avanzo

Photography: Otello Martelli
Cameramen: Carlo Carlini, Gianni Di Venanzo, Carlo Di Palma
Editing: Eraldo Da Roma
Music: Renzo Rossellini
Sound: Ovidio Del Grande
Producer: Mario Conti and Roberto Rossellini for the Organizzazione Film Internazionali, with the collaboration of Rod E. Geiger for Foreign Film Production
Cast: Episode 1 (Sicily): Carmela Sazio (Carmela); Robert Van Loon (Joe from Jersey); Benjamin Emmanuel, Raymond Campbell, Merlin Berth, Mats Carlson, Leonard Penish (American soldiers); Harold Wagner, Albert Heinze (German soldiers); Carlo Pisacane (old man). Episode 2 (Naples): Dots M. Johnson (Joe, a soldier); Alfonsino Pasca (Pasquale); Pippo Bonazzi. Episode 3 (Rome): Gar Moore (Fred); Maria Michi (Francesca); Lorena Berg (Sora Amalia, owner of the pensione). Episode 4 (Florence): Harriet White (Harriet, the American nurse); Renzo Avanzo (Massimo); Gigi Gori (Gigi, a partisan); Gianfranco Corsini (Marco, another partisan); Giulietta Masina (a girl on the stairs); Renato Campos (the major on the roof). Episode 5 (monastery): William Tubbs (Captain Bill Martin); Newell Jones (Captain Jones); Elmer Feldman (Captain Feldman); and the participation of the Franciscan monks from the monastery at Maiori near Salerno. Episode 6 (Porto Tolle, on the Po delta): Dale Edmonds (Dale, the OAS liaison officer); Cigolani (himself); Roberto Van Loel (the German officer); Alan and Dane (two American soldiers). Voice-over: Giulio Panicali
Length: 126 minutes
First screening or transmission (if intended for television): Venice, 18 September 1946
Awards: ANICA Cup (Venice Biennale, 1946); Silver Ribbon for Best Director, Script, and Music (Italy, 1946–47); New York Film Critics Award for Best Foreign Film (1948); National Board of Review Best Film (1948)

Germania anno zero (Germany, Year Zero). 1947
Subject: Roberto Rossellini, from an idea by Basilio Franchina (not credited)
Screenplay: Roberto Rossellini, Max Colpet, Carlo Lizzani
Assistant directors: Max Colpet, Carlo Lizzani, Count Franz Treuberg (not credited)
Photography: Robert Julliard
Cameramen: Emil Puet, Jacques Robin
Editing: Eraldo Da Roma

Music: Renzo Rossellini
Sound: Kurt Doubrawsky
Set design: Piero Filippone
Producer: Roberto Rossellini; Alfredo Guarini (not credited) for Tevere Film, in collaboration with Salvo D'Angelo Produzione (Rome), Sadfi (Berlin), and Union Générale Cinématographique (Paris)
Cast: Edmund Meschke (Edmund Koehler), Ernst Pittschau (Edmund's father), Ingetraud Hinze (Eva, Edmund's sister), Franz Krüger (Karl-Heinz, Edmund's brother), Erich Gühne (Enning, the schoolteacher), Babsy Reckwell (Joe), Alexandra Manys (Christal), Hans Sangen and Heidi Blänkner (Mr. and Mrs. Rademaker), Barbara Hintz (Thilde), Count Franz Treuberg (General von Laubniz), Karl Krüger (the doctor)
Length: 78 minutes
First screening or transmission (if intended for television): Milan, 1 December 1948
Awards: Best Film and Best Script at Locarno Festival (1948)

L'amore (Love). 1948
Episode 1. *Una voce umana (The Human Voice)*
Subject: La voix humaine by Jean Cocteau
Screenplay: Roberto Rossellini
Photography: Robert Julliard
Editing: Eraldo Da Roma
Music: Renzo Rossellini
Sound: Kurt Doubrawsky
Set design: Christian Bérard
Producer: Roberto Rossellini for Tevere Film
Cast: Anna Magnani (the woman on the telephone)
Length: 35 minutes
Episode 2. *Il miracolo (The Miracle)*
Subject: Federico Fellini, from a story by Ramon María Del Valle-Inclan
Screenplay: Tullio Pinelli, Federico Fellini
Photography: Aldo Tonti
Editing: Eraldo Da Roma
Music: Renzo Rossellini
Sound: Kurt Doubrawsky
Producer: Roberto Rossellini for Tevere Film
Cast: Anna Magnani (Nannina), Federico Fellini (the vagabond), the inhabitants of Amalfi and Maiori

Length: 43 minutes
First screening or transmission (if intended for television): Venice, 21 August 1948

La macchina ammazzacattivi (The Machine to Kill Bad People). 1948–52
Subject: Eduardo De Filippo, Filippo Sarazani
Screenplay: Sergio Amidei, Giancarlo Vigorelli, Franco Brusati, Liana Ferri, Roberto Rossellini (not credited)
Assistant directors: Massimo Mida, Renzo Avanzo
Photography: Tino Santoni
Cameraman: Enrico Betti Berutti
Special effects: Eugenio Bava
Editing: Jolanda Benvenuti
Music: Renzo Rossellini
Sound: Mario Amari
Producer: Roberto Rossellini and Luigi Rovere for Universalia/Tevere Film
Cast: Gennaro Pisano (Celestino Esposito), William and Helen Tubbs (the American couple), Marilyn Buferd (the American girl), Giovanni Amato (the mayor), Joe Falletta (Joe), Giacomo Furia (Romano Cuccurullo), Clara Bindi (Giulietta Del Bello), and others, including the inhabitants of Maiori, Amalfi, and Atrani.
Length: 83 minutes
First screening or transmission (if intended for television): Milan, 20 May 1952

Stromboli, terra di Dio (Stromboli, Land of God). 1949
Subject: Roberto Rossellini
Screenplay: Roberto Rossellini, Art Cohn, with the collaboration of Sergio Amidei, Gian Paolo Callegari, Renzo Cesana, and Father Félix Morlion (not credited)
Assistant director: Marcello Caracciolo di Laurino
Photography: Otello Martelli
Cameramen: Luciano Trasatti, Roberto Gerardi, Ajace Parolin
Editing: Jolanda Benvenuti
Music: Renzo Rossellini
Sound: Terry Kellum, Eraldo Giordani
Producer: Berit Film (Rossellini and Bergman) with RKO
Cast: Ingrid Bergman (Karin Bjorsen), Mario Vitale (Antonio Mastrostefano), Renzo Cesana (the priest), Mario Sponza (lighthouse keeper), and the people of the island of Stromboli

Length: 105 minutes (81 minutes in the cut American version)
First screening or transmission (if intended for television): Milan, 9 March
1951

Francesco, giullare di Dio (The Flowers of St. Francis). 1950
Subject: Roberto Rossellini, from *The Little Flowers of St. Francis* and *The Life of Brother Ginepro*
Screenplay: Roberto Rossellini, Federico Fellini, with the collaboration of Father Félix Morlion and Father Antonio Lisandrini
Assistant director: Gianfranco Parolini
Photography: Otello Martelli
Cameramen: Carlo Carlini, Luciano Trasatti
Editing: Jolanda Benvenuti
Music: Renzo Rossellini, Father Enrico Buondonno
Sound: Eraldo Giordani, Ovidio Del Grande
Set design: Virgilio Marchi, Giuseppe Rissone
Costumes: Marina Arcangeli
Producer: Peppino Amato for Cineriz
Cast: Aldo Fabrizi (the tyrant Nicolaio), Arabella Lemaître (Saint Clare), and a group of Franciscan monks, including Brother Nazario Gerardi (St. Francis)
Length: 75 minutes
First screening or transmission (if intended for television): Milan, 15 December 1950

I sette peccati capitali (The Seven Deadly Sins). 1952. **Episode 5: L'invidia (Envy)**
Subject: Roberto Rossellini, from *La Chatte,* a novella by Colette
Screenplay: Roberto Rossellini, Diego Fabbri, Liana Ferri, Turi Vasile
Photography: Enzo Serafin
Editing: Louisette Hautecoeur
Music: Yves Baudrier
Set design: Hugo Blaetter
Producer: Film Costellazione (Rome) and Franco-London Film (Paris)
Cast: Orfeo Tamburi (Orfeo), Andrée Debar (Camille), Nicola Ciarletta, Nino Franchina, Tanino Chiurazzi, R. M. De Angelis
Length: 20 minutes [the other episodes are by Yves Allégret, Claude Autant-Lara, Carlo Rim, Jean Dreville, Eduardo De Filippo, and Georges Lacombe]
First screening or transmission (if intended for television): Paris, 30 April 1952

Europa '51 (Europa '51). 1952
Subject: Roberto Rossellini, from an idea by Massimo Mida and Antonello Trombadori
Screenplay: Roberto Rossellini, Sandro De Feo, Diego Fabbri, Ivo Perilli, Brunello Rondi, Antonio Pietrangeli, and Mario Pannunzio, with major uncredited contributions by Tullio Pinelli and Federico Fellini
Assistant directors: Antonio Pietrangeli, William Demby
Photography: Aldo Tonti
Editing: Jolanda Benvenuti
Music: Renzo Rossellini
Sound: Piero Cavazzuti, Paolo Uccello
Set design: Virgilio Marchi, Ferdinando Ruffo
Costumes: Fernanda Gattinoni
Producer: Ponti–De Laurentiis
Cast: Ingrid Bergman (Irene Girard), Alexander Knox (George, her husband), Sandro Franchina (Michel, her son), Ettore Giannini (Andrea Casati, the Communist), Giulieta Masina (Giulietta, called "Passerotto"), William Tubbs (Professor Alessandrini), Teresa Pellati (Ines, the prostitute), and many others
Length: 110 minutes
First screening or transmission (if intended for television): Venice, 12 September 1952
Awards: International Prize (Venice Biennale, 1952); Silver Ribbon for Best Female Actress (Italy, 1952–53)

Dov'è la libertà . . . ? (Where Is Liberty . . . ?). 1952–54
Subject: Roberto Rossellini
Screenplay: Vitaliano Brancati, Ennio Flaiano, Antonio Pietangeli, Vincenzo Talarico, Roberto Rossellini
Assistant directors: Marcello Caracciolo, Luigi Giacosi
Photography: Aldo Tonti, Tonino Delli Colli
Editing: Jolanda Benvenuti
Music: Renzo Rossellini
Sound: Paolo Uccello
Set design: Flavio Mogherini, Armando Suscipi
Costumes: Antonelli and Ferroni
Producer: Ponti–De Laurentiis/Golden Films
Cast: Totò (Salvatore Lojacono), Leopoldo Trieste (Abramo Piperno), Vera Molnar (Agnesina), Franca Faldini (Maria), Nyta Dover
Length: 95 minutes

First screening or transmission (if intended for television): Rome, 26 March 1954

Siamo donne (We, the Women). 1953. Episode 3: *Ingrid Bergman*
Subject: Cesare Zavattini
Screenplay: Cesare Zavattini, with the collaboration of Luigi Chiarini
Assistant director: Niccolò Ferrari
Photography: Otello Martelli
Editing: Jolanda Benvenuti
Music: Alessandro Cicognini
Sound: Giorgio Pallotta
Producer: Alfredo Guarini for Titanus/Costellazione
Cast: Ingrid Bergman (as herself); Albamaria Setaccioli (Signora Annovazzi); Robertino, Isabella, and Isotta Rossellini (as themselves)
Length: 20 minutes [other episodes by Alfredo Guarini, Gianni Franciolini, Luigi Zampa, and Luchino Visconti]
First screening or transmission (if intended for television): Milan, 27 October 1953

Viaggio in Italia (Voyage in Italy, also known as The Strangers). 1953
Subject: Roberto Rossellini, Vitaliano Brancati
Screenplay: Roberto Rossellini, Vitaliano Brancati
Photography: Enzo Serafin, assisted by Aldo Tonti and Luciano Trasatti
Camerman: Aldo Scavarda
Editing: Jolanda Benvenuti
Music: Renzo Rossellini
Sound: Eraldo Giordani
Set design: Piero Filippone
Costumes: Fernanda Gattinoni
Producer: Roberto Rossellini for Sveva Film, Aldo Fossataro for Junior Film, Alfredo Guarini for Italian Film/Société Générale de Cinématographie/Ariane/Francinex
Cast: Ingrid Bergman (Katherine Joyce), George Sanders (Alexander Joyce), Paul Müller (Paul Dupont), Maria Mauban (Marie), Anna Proclemer (the prostitute), Leslie Daniels (Tony Burton), Natalia Ray (Natalia Burton), Tony La Penna (Bartolo), Jackie Frost (Judy), Lyla Rocco (Mrs. Sinibaldi), Bianca Maria Cerasoli (Judy's friend)
Length: 75 minutes
First screening or transmission (if intended for television): Milan, 7 September 1954

Amori di mezzo secolo (Mid-Century Loves). 1953. Episode 4: *Napoli 1943 (Naples 1943)*
Subject: Carlo Infascelli
Screenplay: Oreste Biancoli, Roberto Rossellini, Vinicio Marinucci, Giuseppe Mangione, Rodolfo Sonego
Photography: Tonino Delli Colli
Editing: Jolanda Benvenuti, Dolores Tamburini
Music: Carlo Rustichelli
Set design: Mario Chiari, Beni Montresor
Costumes: Maria De Matteis
Producer: Carlo Infascelli for Excelsa/Roma Film
Cast: Antonella Lualdi (Carla), Franco Pastorino (Renato), Ugo D'Alessio (an actor)
Length: 15 minutes [other episodes by Glauco Pellegrini, Pietro Germi, Mario Chiari, and Antonio Pietrangeli]
First screening or transmission (if intended for television): Milan, 18 February 1954

Giovanna d'Arco al rogo (Joan of Arc at the Stake). 1954
Subject: From the dramatic oratorio, *Jeanne au bûcher,* by Paul Claudel and Arthur Honegger
Screenplay: Roberto Rossellini
Photography: Gabor Pogany
Editing: Jolanda Benvenuti
Music: Arthur Honegger
Sound: Paolo Uccello
Set design: Carlo Maria Cristini, Marcello Caracciolo Di Laurino
Costumes: Adriano Muojo
Producer: Giorgio Criscuolo and Franco Francese for Produzioni Cinematografiche Associate and Franco-London Film
Cast: Ingrid Bergman (Joan of Arc), Tullio Carminati (Brother Domenico), Giacinto Prandelli (Porcus), Augusto Romani (the giant, Heurtebise), Agnese Dubbini (Signora Botti)
Length: 76 minutes
First screening or transmission (if intended for television): Milan, 29 January 1955

La paura (non credo più all'amore) (Fear, also known as Angst). 1954
Subject: Stefan Zweig's novella, *Die Angst*
Screenplay: Sergio Amidei, Roberto Rossellini, Count Franz Treuberg

Assistant directors: Pietro Servadio, Count Franz Treuberg
Photography: Carlo Carlini, Heinz Schnackertz
Editing: Jolanda Benvenuti, Walter Boos
Music: Renzo Rossellini
Sound: Carl Becker
Costumes: Jacques Griffe
Producer: Ariston Film/Aniene Film
Cast: Ingrid Bergman (Irene Wagner), Mathias Wieman (Albert Wagner), Kurt Kreuger (Enrico Stoltz), Renate Mannhardt (Johanna Schultze/Luisa Vidor), Klaus Kinski
Length: 83 minutes
First screening or transmission (if intended for television): Hamburg, 5 November 1954

Le psychodrame (Psychodrama). 1956
Photography: Roberto Rossellini
Producer: ORTF (France). (French state television)
[Documentary film begun in 1956 but never completed]

L'India vista da Rossellini (India Seen by Rossellini). 1957–58
[A 16-millimeter, 10-episode, 251-minute version of the material later edited to four episodes and 90 minutes as *India*]
Television Supervision: Giuseppe Sala
Photography: Aldo Tonti
Producer: Roberto Rossellini for the RAI-TV (Italian state television)
Cast: Nonprofessionals
Length: 251 minutes
First screening or transmission (if intended for television): RAI-TV, Programma Nazionale; 7 January through 11 March 1959

India, also known as *India, Matri Bhumi (India, Mother Earth).* 1958
Subject: Roberto Rossellini
Screenplay: Roberto Rossellini, Sonali Senroy Das Gupta, Fereydoun Hoveyda
Assistant directors: Tinto Brass, Jean Herman
Photography: Aldo Tonti
Editing: Cesare Cavagna
Music: Philippe Arthuys
Producer: Aniene Film and Union Générale Cinématographique
Cast: Nonprofessional actors

163

Length: 90 minutes
First screening or transmission (if intended for television): Milan, 12 March 1960

J'ai fait un beau voyage (I Had a Fine Trip). 1959
[A French version of the Italian *L'India vista da Rossellini;* Rossellini is interviewed by Etienne Lalou; the program is presented in 10 episodes]
First screening or transmission (if intended for television): ORTF (French state television); January through August 1959

Il generale Della Rovere (General Della Rovere). 1959
Subject: Indro Montanelli
Screenplay: Sergio Amidei, Diego Fabbri, Indro Montanelli, Roberto Rossellini, Piero Zuffi
Assistant directors: Tinto Brass, Philippe Arthuys, Renzo Rossellini, Jr.
Photography: Carlo Carlini
Editing: Cesare Cavagna
Music: Renzo Rossellini
Sound: Ovidio Del Grande
Set design: Piero Zuffi
Costumes: Piero Zuffi
Producer: Morris Ergas for Zebra Film and Gaumont
Cast: Vittorio De Sica (Emanuele Bardone, alias Colonel Grimaldi, alias General Giovanni Braccioforte Della Rovere), Hannes Messemer (Colonel Müller), Sandra Milo (Olga), Giovanna Ralli (Valeria), Anne Vernon (Carla Fassio), Vittorio Caprioli (Aristide Banchelli), Giuseppe Rossetti (Fabrizio), Lucia Modugno (a partisan), Herbert Fischer (Walter Hageman), Franco Interlenghi (Antonio Pasquali), and many others
Length: 133 minutes
First screening or transmission (if intended for television): Venice, 31 August 1959
Awards: Golden Lion (Venice Biennale, 1959); Best Film, Direction, Script, Leading Actor, and Supporting Actor (San Francisco Film Festival, 1960); Blue Ribbon for Best Director (Italy, 1960); David di Donatello Award for Best Production (Italy, 1959–60); Second-Best Foreign Film by both the National Board of Review and the New York Film Critics (New York, 1960)

Era notte a Roma (It Was Night in Rome). 1960
Subject: Sergio Amidei

Screenplay: Sergio Amidei, Diego Fabbri, Brunello Rondi, Roberto Rossellini, Mario Del Papa (English dialogue)
Assistant directors: Renzo Rossellini, Jr.; Franco Rossellini
Photography: Carlo Carlini
Editing: Roberto Cinquini
Music: Renzo Rossellini
Sound: Enzo Magli
Set design: Flavio Mogherini, Mario Rappini
Costumes: Elio Costanzi, Marcella De Marchis
Producer: Giovanbattista Romanengo for International Golden Star/Film Dismage
Cast: Leo Genn (Major Mike Pemberton), Giovanna Ralli (Esperia Belli), Sergei Bondartchuk (Sergeant Fjodor Nazukov), Peter Baldwin (Lt. Peter Bradley), Renato Salvatori (Renato), Paolo Stoppa (Prince Alessandro Antoniani), Enrico Maria Salerno (Doctor Costanzi), Hannes Messemer (Colonel von Kleist), Laura Betti (Teresa), Sergio Fantoni (Don Valerio), George Petrarca (Tarcisio)
Length: 136 minutes
First screening or transmission (if intended for television): Cannes, 13 May 1960

Viva l'Italia (Garibaldi). 1960
Subject: Sergio Amidei, Carlo Alianello, Antonio Petrucci, Luigi Chiarini
Screenplay: Sergio Amidei, Diego Fabbri, Antonio Petrucci, Roberto Rossellini, Antonello Trombadori
Assistant directors: Renzo Rossellini, Jr.; Franco Rossellini; Ruggero Deodato
Photography: Luciano Trasatti
Editing: Roberto Cinquini
Music: Renzo Rossellini
Sound: Enzo Magli, Oscar Di Santo
Set design: Gepy Mariani
Costumes: Marcella De Marchis
Producer: Cineriz/Tempo Film/Galatea/Zebra/Francinex
Cast: Renzo Ricci (Giuseppe Garibaldi), Paolo Stoppa (Nino Bixio), Franco Interlenghi (Giuseppe Bandi), Giovanna Ralli (Rosa), Tina Louise (French journalist), and numerous others
Length: 128 minutes
First screening or transmission (if intended for television): Rome, 27 January 1961

Vanina Vanini (Vanina Vanini). 1961
Subject: Stendhal's *Chroniques italiennes,* adapted by Antonello Trombadori and Franco Solinas
Screenplay: Roberto Rossellini, Diego Fabbri, Jean Gruault, Monique Lange
Assistant directors: Renzo Rossellini, Jr.; Franco Rossellini; Philippe Arthuys
Photography: Luciano Trasatti
Editing: Daniele Alabiso, Mario Serandrei
Music: Renzo Rossellini
Sound: Oscar De Angelis, Renato Cadueri
Set design: Luigi Scaccianoce, Riccardo Domenici
Costumes: Danilo Donati
Producer: Morris Ergas for Zebra Film and Orsay Film
Cast: Sandra Milo (Vanina Vanini), Laurent Terzieff (Pietro Missirilli), Paolo Stoppa (Prince Asdrubale Vanini), Martine Carol (Countess Vitelleschi), Leonardo Botta (Vanina's confessor), Nerio Bernardi (Cardinal Savelli), and others
Length: 127 minutes
First screening or transmission (if intended for television): Venice, 27 August 1961

Torino nei cent'anni (Turin through the Last Hundred Years). 1961
[Television documentary on the history of the city from 1860 to 1960]
Subject: Valentino Orsini
Screenplay: Valentino Orsini
Photography: Leopoldo Piccinelli, Mario Vulpiani, Mario Volpe
Editing: Vasco Micucci
Producer: PROA for the RAI-TV (Italian state television)
Length: 46 minutes
First screening or transmission (if intended for television): RAI-TV, Programma Nazionale; 10 September 1961

Anima nera (Black Soul). 1962
Subject: Adapted from the comedy of the same title by Giuseppe Patroni Griffi
Screenplay: Roberto Rossellini, Giuseppe Patroni Griffi, Alfio Valdarnini
Assistant directors: Franco Rossellini, Ruggero Deodato
Photography: Luciano Trasatti
Editing: Daniele Alabiso
Music: Piero Piccioni

Set design: Elio Costanzi, Alfredo Freda
Costumes: Marcella De Marchis
Producer: Gianni Hecht Lucari for Documento Film/Le Louvre Film
Cast: Vittorio Gassman (Adriano), Annette Stroyberg (Marcella), Nadja Tiller (Mimosa), Eleonora Rossi Drago (Alessandra), Yvonne Sanson (Olga), Daniela Igliozzi (Giovanna), Tony Brown (Guidino)
Length: 97 minutes
First screening or transmission (if intended for television): Milan, 5 September 1962

Rogopag (Rogopag). Episode 1: *Illibatezza (Chastity).* 1962
Subject: Roberto Rossellini
Screenplay: Roberto Rossellini
Assistant director: Renzo Rossellini, Jr.
Photography: Luciano Trasatti
Editing: Daniele Alabiso
Music: Carlo Rustichelli
Sound: Bruno Brunacci, Luigi Puri
Set design: Flavio Mogherini
Costumes: Danilo Donati
Producer: Alfredo Bini for Arco Film/Lyre Cinématographique
Cast: Rosanna Schiaffino (Anna Maria), Bruce Balaban (Joe), Carlo Zappavigna (Anna Maria's fiancé), Maria Pia Schiaffino (a hostess)
Length: 33 minutes [the other episodes were directed by Jean-Luc Godard, Pier Paolo Pasolini, and Ugo Gregoretti]
First screening or transmission (if intended for television): Milan, 21 February 1963

L'età del ferro (The Iron Age). 1964
[Directed by Renzo Rossellini, Jr., with the supervision of Roberto Rossellini for Italian state television]
Subject: Roberto Rossellini
Screenplay: Roberto Rossellini
Photography: Carlo Carlini
Editing: Daniele Alabiso
Music: Carmine Rizzo
Sound: Renato Cadueri, Pietro Spadoni
Set design: Giuseppe Mariani, Ennio Michettoni
Costumes: Marcella De Marchis
Producer: 22 Dicembre and Istituto Luce for RAI-TV

Cast: Nonprofessionals
Length: 5 episodes of approximately 55–60 minutes each
First screening or transmission (if intended for television): RAI-TV, Channel Two; 19 February through 19 March 1965

La prise de pouvoir par Louis XIV (The Rise to Power of Louis XIV). 1966
Subject: Philippe Erlanger
Screenplay: Philippe Erlanger, with dialogues by Jean Gruault
Assistant directors: Yves Kovacs, Egérie Mavraki
Photography: Georges Leclerc
Special effects: Marc Schmidt, Bernard Cinquin, Jean Faivre
Editing: Armand Ridel
Music: Betty Willemetz
Sound: Jacques Gayet
Set design: Maurice Valay, Pierre Gerber
Costumes: Christiane Coste, Pierre Cadot
Producer: Radiodiffusion Française (ORTF—French state television).
Cast: Jean-Marie Patte (Louis XIV), Raymond Jourdan (Colbert), Katharina Renn (Anne of Austria), Giulio Cesare Silvagni (Mazarin), Dominique Vincent (Madame du Plessis), Pierre Barrat (Fouquet), and many others
Length: 102 minutes
First screening or transmission (if intended for television): Venice, 1966 September (first screen presentation); first Italian television presentation on RAI-TV, Programma Nazionale, 23 April 1967

Idea di un'isola (Roberto Rossellini's Sicily). 1967
Subject: Roberto Rossellini
Screenplay: Roberto Rossellini
Photography: Mario Fioretti
Editing: Maria Rosada
Music: Mario Nascimbene
Producer: Renzo Rossellini, Jr., for Orizzonte 2000, in collaboration with the RAI-TV for NBC Television
Length: 60 minutes
First screening or transmission (if intended for television): NBC Television, 1968; RAI-TV, Channel Two, 3 February 1970

La lotta dell'uomo per la sua sopravvivenza (Man's Struggle for Survival). 1967–69
[Directed by Renzo Rossellini, Jr., with the supervision of Roberto Rossellini]

Subject: Roberto Rossellini
Screenplay: Roberto Rossellini
Photography: Mario Fioretti
Editing: Daniele Alabiso, Gabriele Alessandro, Alfredo Muschietti
Music: Mario Nascimbene
Set design: Giuseppe Mariani, Virgil Moise, Ennio Michettoni, Giusto Puri Purini, Eugenio Saverio, Jurie Vasile
Costumes: Marcella De Marchis
Producer: RAI-TV and Orrizonte 2000/Logos Film/Romania Film/Corpo Film
Cast: Nonprofessionals
Length: 12 episodes of approximately 50–60 minutes each
First screening or transmission (if intended for television): RAI-TV, Channel One, 4 August through 11 September 1970 (Episodes 1–6); RAI-TV, Channel Two, 4 September through 16 October 1971 (Episodes 7–12)

Atti degli apostoli *(The Acts of the Apostles),* 1968
Subject: Acts of the Apostles, the fifth book of the New Testament
Screenplay: Vittorio Bonicelli, Jean-Dominique de la Rochefoucauld, Roberto Rossellini, Luciano Scaffa
Photography: Mario Fioretti
Editing: Jolanda Benvenuti
Music: Mario Nascimbene
Sound: Gianni Mazzarini
Set Design: Giuseppe Mariani, Carmelo Patrono, Elio Costanzi, Alessandro Gioia, Dino Leonetto
Costumes: Marcella De Marchis
Producer: Renzo Rossellini, Jr., for Orizzonte 2000/RAI-TV/ORTF/TVE Madrid/Studio Hamburg/Les Films de Carthage (Tunisia)
Cast: Edoardo Torricella (Paul), Jacques Dumur (Peter), Renzo Rossi (Zacharias), Mohamed Kouka (John), Bradai Ridha (Matthew), and many others
Length: 5 episodes of 58, 58, 64, 64, and 98 minutes
First screening or transmission (if intended for television): RAI-TV, Programma Nazionale; 6 April through 4 May 1969

Socrate *(Socrates).* 1970
Subject: Adapted from the *Dialogues* of Plato by Roberto Rossellini and Maria Grazia Bornigia

Screenplay: Roberto Rossellini, Marcella Mariani, with dialogues by Jean-Dominique de la Rochefoucauld
Assistant directors: Juan Garcia Atienza, José Luis Guarner
Photography: Jorge Herrero Martin
Editing: Alfredo Muschietti
Music: Mario Nascimbene
Sound: Jesus Paralta Navarro
Set design: Giusto Puri Purini, Bernardo Ballester
Costumes: Marcella De Marchis
Producer: Orizzonte 2000/RAI-TV/ORTF/TVE Madrid
Cast: Jean Sylvère (Socrates), Anne Caprile (Xanthippe), Ricardo Palacios (Criton), Bepy Mannajuolo (Apollodorus), and many others
Length: 120 minutes
First screening or transmission (if intended for television): Venice, 19 August 1970; RAI-TV, Channel One, 17 and 20 June 1971

La forza e la ragione (Intervista a Salvatore Allende) (Force and Reason [Interview with Salvador Allende]). 1971
[An interview conducted in May 1971 by Rossellini, with the assistance of Emilio Greco]
Photography: Roberto Girometti
Sound: Antonio Russello
Producer: Orizzonte 2000
Length: 36 minutes
First screening or transmission (if intended for television): RAI-TV, Channel One; 15 September 1973 (after the news of Allende's death).

Rice University. 1971
[A documentary on Rice University that was never completed]
Editing: Beppe Cino
Producer: Orizzonte 2000
Length: 2 episodes of about 50 minutes each

Blaise Pascal. 1972
Subject: Roberto Rossellini, Marcella Mariani, Luciano Scaffa
Screenplay: Roberto Rossellini, Marcella Mariani, Luciano Scaffa, with dialogues by Jean-Dominique de la Rochefoucauld
Photography: Mario Fioretti
Editing: Jolanda Benvenuti
Music: Mario Nascimbene

170

Sound: Carlo Tarchi
Set design: Franco Velchi
Costumes: Marcella De Marchis, with the collaboration of Isabella Rossellini
Producer: Roberto Rossellini for Orizzonte 2000/RAI-TV/ORTF
Cast: Pierre Arditi (Blaise Pascal), Giuseppe Addobbati (Etienne Pascal), Rita Forzano (Jacqueline Pascal), Teresa Ricci (Gilberte Pascal), Claude Baks (Descartes), Tullio Valli (Father Mersenne), and many others
Length: 131 minutes
First screening or transmission (if intended for television): RAI-TV, Channel One; 16 and 17 May 1972

Agostino d'Ippona (Augustine of Hippo). 1972
Subject: Roberto Rossellini, Marcella Mariani, Luciano Scaffa
Screenplay: Roberto Rossellini, Marcella Mariani, Luciano Scaffa, with dialogues by Jean-Dominique de la Rochefoucauld
Photography: Mario Fioretti
Editing: Jolanda Benvenuti
Music: Mario Nascimbene
Sound: Carlo Tarchi
Set design: Franco Velchi
Costumes: Marcella De Marchis, with the collaboration of Isabella Rossellini
Producer: Roberto Rossellini for Orizzonte 2000/RAI-TV
Cast: Dary Berkany (Augustine), Virginio Gazzolo (Alypius), Cesare Barbetti (Volusianus), Bruno Cattaneo (Maximus), Leonardo Fioravanti (Milesius), Bepy Mannajuolo (Severus), and many others
Length: 171 minutes
First screening or transmission (if intended for television): Turin, 19 September 1972; RAI-TV, Channel One, 25 October through 1 November 1972

L'età di Cosimo de' Medici (The Age of the Medici). 1972
Subject: Roberto Rossellini, Marcella Mariani, Luciano Scaffa
Screenplay: Roberto Rossellini, Marcella Mariani, Luciano Scaffa
Photography: Mario Montuori
Editing: Jolanda Benvenuti
Music: Manuel De Sica
Sound: Carlo Tarchi
Set design: Franco Velchi, Ezio Di Monte

Costumes: Marcella De Marchis
Producer: Roberto Rossellini for Orizzonte 2000/RAI-TV
Cast: Marcello Di Falco (Cosimo de' Medici); Virginio Gazzolo (Leon Battista Alberti); Tom Felleghi (Rinaldo degli Albizzi); Mario Erpichini (Totto Machiavelli); and numerous others
Length: 3 episodes of 250 minutes
First screening or transmission (if intended for television): RAI-TV, Channel One; 26 December 1972 through 9 January 1973

Cartesio (Descartes). 1973
Subject: Roberto Rossellini, Marcella Mariani, Luciano Scaffa
Screenplay: Roberto Rossellini, Marcella Mariani, Luciano Scaffa, with the assistance of Ferdinand Alquié
Photography: Mario Montuori
Editing: Jolanda Benvenuti
Music: Mario Nascimbene
Sound: Tommaso Quattrini
Set design: Giuseppe Mangano
Costumes: Marcella De Marchis
Producer: Roberto Rossellini for Orizzonte 2000/RAI-TV/ORTF
Cast: Ugo Cardea (Descartes), Anne Pouchie (Elena), Claude Berthy (Guez de Balzac), Gabriele Banchero (Bretagne), John Stacy (Levasseur d'Etoiles), Charles Borromel (Father Mersenne), and many others
Length: 150 minutes
First screening or transmission (if intended for television): RAI-TV, Channel One; 20–27 February 1974

Anno uno (Italy: Year One). 1974
Subject: Roberto Rossellini, Marcella Mariani, Luciano Scaffa
Screenplay: Roberto Rossellini, Marcella Mariani, Luciano Scaffa
Photography: Mario Montuori
Editing: Jolanda Benvenuti
Music: Mario Nascimbene
Sound: Tommaso Quattrini, Franco De Arcangelis
Set design: Giuseppe Mangano
Costumes: Marcella De Marchis
Producer: Rusconi Film
Cast: Luigi Vannucchi (Alcide De Gasperi), Dominique Darel (Maria Romana De Gasperi), Valeria Sabel (Francesca De Gasperi), Ennio Balbo (Nenni), Tino Bianchi (Palmiro Togliatti), Francesco Di Federico (Saragat),

172

Luciano Gaudenzio (Longo), Paolo Bonacelli (Amendola), and many others
Length: 118 minutes
First screening or transmission (if intended for television): Rome, 15 November 1974

The World Population. 1974
[A documentary filmed by Rossellini, with the assistance of Beppe Cino, for the United Nations]
Length: 120 minutes
First screening or transmission (if intended for television): Bucharest, 1974; subsequently distributed by UNESCO around the world

Il Messia (The Messiah). 1975
Subject: Roberto Rossellini, Silvia D'Amico Bendicò
Screenplay: Roberto Rossellini, Silvia D'Amico Bendicò
Photography: Mario Montuori
Editing: Jolanda Benvenuti
Music: Mario Nascimbene
Sound: Alain Contrault, Tommaso Quattrini
Set design: Giorgio Bertolini, Giovanni Del Drago, Osvaldo Desideri
Costumes: Marcella De Marchis
Producer: Silvia D'Amico Bendicò for Orizzonte 2000/Procinex-FR3-Telefilm Production
Cast: Pier Maria Rossi (Jesus Christ), Mita Ungaro (Mary), Carlos de Cavahlho (John the Baptist), Yatsugi Khelil (Joseph), Jean Martin (Pontius Pilate), and many others
Length: 145 minutes
First screening or transmission (if intended for television): Montecatini, 25 October 1975

Concerto per Michelangelo (Concert for Michelangelo). 1977
[Rossellini explores the frescoes in the Sistine Chapel during a concert by the chorus of the Cappella Musicale Pontificia directed by Monsignor Domenico Bartolucci]
Photography: Mario Montuori
Sound: Vincenzo Sirena
Producer: RAI-TV, Channel 2
Length: Approximately 60 minutes
First screening or transmission (if intended for television): 9 April 1977

Beaubourg, Centre d'Art et de Culture Georges Pompidou (Beaubourg, the Georges Pompidou Center for Art and Culture). 1977
[A documentary on the Beaubourg Museum]
Photography: Nestor Almendros
Editing: Véritable Silve, Colette Le Tallec, Dominique Taysse
Sound: Philippe Lémenuel, Michel Brethex
Producer: Création 9 Information–Film Jacques Grandclaude
Length: 57 minutes [Rossellini was apparently going to make some changes in this documentary before his death on 3 June 1977; shooting was completed on 6 May 1977]
First screening or transmission (if intended for television): RAI-TV, Channel Three; 1 October 1983

Current U.S. Rental Information of 16-Millimeter Prints or Videocassettes

L'uomo dalla croce: Facets, Inc.
Roma città aperta: Budget; Corinth; Images; Kit Parker; Liberty; Facets, Inc.; Tamarelle's International Films
Paisà: Budget; Films, Inc.; Images; Kit Parker; Facets, Inc.; Tamarelle's International Films
Germania anno zero: Films, Inc.; Facets, Inc.; Speedimpex; Tamarelle's International Films
L'amore: Films, Inc.; Facets, Inc.; Tamarelle's International Films
La macchina ammazzacattivi: Films, Inc.
Stromboli: Budget; Films, Inc.; Kit Parker; Liberty; Facets, Inc.; Tamarelle's International Films
Francesco, giullare di Dio: Facets, Inc.
Viaggio in Italia: Films, Inc.; Images; Facets, Inc.; Tamarelle's International Films
La paura: Films, Inc.; Facets, Inc.
Il generale Della Rovere: Budget; New Yorker; Facets, Inc.
Era notte a Roma: Films, Inc.
Viva l'Italia: Liberty
Vanina Vanini: Corinth; Facets, Inc.
Rogopag: Films, Inc.
La prise de pouvoir par Louis XIV: Museum of Modern Art; New Yorker; Facets, Inc.; Tamarelle's International Films

Film distributors in the rental list are given in alphabetical order; most videocassettes are available from either Facets, Inc., or Tamarelle's International Films. If videocassettes are available, the distributor is listed after available sources for 16-millimeter prints. When a film is not listed, it is currently unavailable in either of the two formats in the United States.

Socrate: New Yorker
Blaise Pascal: Facets, Inc.
Agostino d'Ippona: Facets, Inc.
L'età di Cosimo de' Medici: Films, Inc.; Facets, Inc.
Il Messia: Facets, Inc.

Bibliography

Aprà, Adriano, ed. *Rosselliniana: bibliografia internazionale, dossier "Paisà."* Rome: Di Giacomo Editore, 1987 [contains a complete international Rossellini bibliography].

Aprà, Adriano, Giuseppe Ghigi, and Patrizia Pistagnesi, eds. *Cinquant'anni di cinema a Venezia.* Venice: Edizioni RAI, 1982.

Aprà, Adriano, and Patrizia Pistagnesi, eds. *The Fabulous Thirties: Italian Cinema, 1929–1944.* Milan: Electra International, 1979.

Aristarco, Guido. *Neorealismo e nuova critica cinematografica: cinematografia e vita nazionale negli anni quaranta e cinquanta: tra rotture e tradizioni.* Florence: Nuova Guaraldi Editrice, 1980.

Armes, Roy. *Patterns of Realism: A Study of Italian Neo-Realism.* Cranbury, N.J.: A. S. Barnes, 1971.

Baldelli, Pio. *Roberto Rossellini: i suoi film (1936–1972) e la filmografia completa.* Rome: Edizioni Samonà e Savelli, 1972.

Baudy, Leo, and Morris Dickstein, eds. *Great Film Directors: A Critical Anthology.* New York: Oxford University Press, 1978.

Bazin, André. *Qu'est-ce que le cinéma?—IV. Une esthétique de la réalité: le néo-réalisme.* Paris: Editions du Cerf, 1962.

What Is Cinema? Volume II. Translated by Hugh Gray. Berkeley and Los Angeles: University of California Press, 1971 [contains many of the essays in the French edition].

Bergman, Ingrid, with Alan Burgess, *My Story.* New York: Delacorte, 1980.

Bizzari, Libero. *Il cinema italiano: industria, mercato, pubblico.* Rome: Edizioni Gulliver, 1987.

Bizzari, Libero, and Libero Solaroli. *L'industria cinematografica italiana.* Florence: Parenti Editore, 1958.

Bohne, Luciana. "Rossellini's *Viaggio in Italia:* A Variation on a Theme by Joyce." *Film Criticism* 3, no. 2 (1979), 43–52.

Bondanella, Peter. "America and the Post-War Italian Cinema." *Rivista di studi italiani* 2 (1984), 106–25.

The Cinema of Federico Fellini. Preface by Federico Fellini. Princeton: Princeton University Press, 1992.

"Course File: Italian Cinema from Neorealism to the Present." *The American Film Institute Education Newsletter* 6 (1983), 4–10. Reprinted in Patricia Erens, *College Course Files*, pp. 104–9. University Film and Video Association, Monograph no. 5. 1986.

Italian Cinema: From Neorealism to the Present. 2d rev. ed. New York: Continuum, 1990.

"Italy." In William Luhr, ed., *World Cinema since 1945*, pp. 349–79. New York: Ungar, 1987.

"Neorealist Aesthetics and the Fantastic: *The Machine to Kill Bad People* and *Miracle in Milan*." *Film Criticism* 3, no. 2 (1979), 24–29.

Bondanella, Peter, ed. *Federico Fellini: Essays in Criticism*. New York: Oxford University Press, 1978.

Brosnian, John. *Movie Magic: The Story of Special Effects in the Cinema*. New York: New American Library, 1976.

Brunetta, Gian Piero. *Storia del cinema italiano, 1895–1945*. Rome: Editori Riuniti, 1979.

Storia del cinema italiano dal 1945 agli anni ottanta. Rome: Editori Riuniti, 1982.

Brunette, Peter. "Just How Brechtian Is Rossellini?" *Film Criticism* 3, no. 2 (1979), 30–42.

Roberto Rossellini. New York: Oxford University Press, 1987.

"Rossellini and Cinematic Realism." *Cinema Journal* 25, no. 1 (1985), 34–49.

"Unity and Difference in *Paisan*." *Studies in the Literary Imagination* 1 (1983), 91–111.

"Visual Motifs in Rossellini's *Viaggio in Italia*." In Peter Lehman, ed., *Close Viewings: An Anthology of New Film Criticism*, pp. 39–56. Tallahassee: Florida State University Press, 1990.

Bruno, Edoardo, ed. *R. R. Roberto Rossellini*. Rome: Bulzoni Editore, 1979.

Burgoyne, Robert. "The Imaginary and the Neo-Real." *Enclitic* 3, no. 1 (1979), 16–34.

Cardillo, Massimo. *Il Duce in moviola: politica e divismo nei cinegiornali e documentari "Luce."* Bari: Edizioni Dedalo, 1983.

Carrano, Patrizia. *La Magnani: il romanzo di una vita*. Preface by Federico Fellini. Milan: Rizzoli, 1986.

Chiarini, Luigi. *Un leone e altri animali: cinema e contestazione alla Mostra di Venezia 1968*. Preface by Jean Renoir. Milan: Sugar Editore, 1969.

Del Buono, Oreste, and Lietta Tornabuoni, eds. *Era Cinecittà: vita, morte e miracoli di una fabbrica di film*. Milan: Bompiani, 1979.

De Santis, Giuseppe. *Verso il neorealismo: un critico cinematografico degli anni quaranta*. Edited by Callisto Cosulich. Rome: Bulzoni Editori, 1982.

Di Giammatteo, Fernaldo. *Roberto Rossellini*. Florence: La Nuova Italia, 1990.

Di Monte, Ezio, et al., eds. *La città del cinema (produzione e lavoro nel cinema italiano, 1930/1970)*. Rome: Editrice R. Napoleone, 1979.

Draper, Ellen. " 'Controversy Has Probably Destroyed Forever the Context': *The Miracle* and Movie Censorship in America in the Fifties." *The Velvet Light Trap* 25 (1990), 69–79.

Ellwood, David. "Italy: The Regime, the Nation, and the Film Industry: An Introduction." In K. R. M. Short, ed., *Film and Radio Propaganda in World War II*, pp. 220–29. Knoxville: University of Tennessee Press, 1983.

Faldini, Franca, and Goffredo Fofi, eds. *L'avventurosa storia del cinema italiano raccontata dai suoi protagonisti, 1935–1959*. Milan: Feltrinelli, 1979.

L'avventurosa storia del cinema italiano raccontata dai suoi protagonisti, 1960–1969. Milan: Feltrinelli, 1981.

Il cinema italiano d'oggi 1970–1984 raccontato dai suoi protagonisti. Milan: Mondadori, 1984.

Farassino, Alberto, ed. *Neorealismo: cinema italiano, 1945–1949*. Turin: EDI, 1989.

Fellini, Federico. *Fare un film*. Turin: Einaudi, 1976.

"The Road beyond Neorealism." In Richard Dyer MacCann, ed., *Film: A Montage of Theories*, pp. 377–84. New York: Dutton, 1966.

"La Strada": Federico Fellini, Director. Edited by Peter Bondanella and Manuela Gieri. New Brunswick, N.J.: Rutgers University Press, 1987.

Freddi, Luigi. *Il cinema*. 2 vols. Rome: L'Arnia, 1949.

Furno, Mariella, and Renzo Renzi, eds. *Il neorealismo nel fascismo: Giuseppe De Santis e la critica cinematografica, 1941–1943*. Bologna: Edizioni della Tipografia Compositori, 1984.

Gallagher, Tag. "NR = MC²: Rossellini, Neo-Realism, and Croce." *Film History* 2, no. 1 (1988), 87–97.

Germani, Sergio G., and Vittorio Martinelli, eds. *Il cinema di Augusto Genina*. Paisan di Prato: Edizioni Biblioteca dell'Immagine, 1989.

Gregor, A. James. *The Ideology of Fascism: The Rationale of Totalitarianism*. New York: Free Press, 1969.

Interpretations of Fascism. Morristown, N.J.: General Learning Press, 1974.

Young Mussolini and the Intellectual Origins of Fascism. Berkeley and Los Angeles: University of California Press, 1979.

Guarner, José Luis. *Roberto Rossellini*. Translated by Elisabeth Cameron. New York: Praeger, 1970.

Hay, James. *Italian Film Culture in Fascist Italy: The Passing of the Rex*. Bloomington: Indiana University Press, 1987.

Hiller, Jim, ed. *Cahiers du Cinéma—The 1950s: Neo-Realism, Hollywood, New Wave*. Cambridge: Harvard University Press, 1985 [articles by Bazin, Ayfre, Rivette, Rohmer, Truffaut, and others on Italian cinema].

Hochkofler, Matilde. *Anna Magnani*. Rome: Gremese Editore, 1984.

Hughes, John. "Recent Rossellini." *Film Comment* 10, no. 4 (1974), 16–21.

Kolker, Robert Phillip. *The Altering Eye: Contemporary International Cinema*. New York: Oxford University Press, 1983.

Landy, Marcia. *Fascism in Film: The Italian Commercial Cinema, 1931–1943*. Princeton: Princeton University Press, 1986.

Laura, Ernesto G. *L'immagine bugiarda: mass-media e spettacolo nella Repubblica di Salò (1943–1945)*. Rome: ANCCI, 1987.

Laura, Ernesto G., ed. *Tutti i film di Venezia, 1932–1984*. 2 vols. Venice: La Biennale, 1985.

Lawton, Ben. "Italian Neorealism: A Mirror Construction of Reality." *Film Criticism* 3, no. 2 (1979), 8–23.

Lyttelton, Adrian, ed. *Italian Fascisms: From Pareto to Gentile*. London: Jonathan Cape, 1973.

MacBean, James Roy. *Film and Revolution*. Bloomington: Indiana University Press, 1975.

Magrelli, Enrico, ed. *Sull'industria cinematografica italiana*. Venice: Marsilio Editori, 1986.

Mancini, Elaine. *Struggles of the Italian Film Industry during Fascism, 1930–1935*. Ann Arbor: University of Michigan Research Press, 1985.

Marchetti, Bianca Maria, and Daniela Niccolini. "Per una definizione della struttura stilistica del realismo di Roberto Rossellini." *Studi Urbinati* 55, no. 3 (1981–82), 239–57.

Marcus, Millicent. *Italian Film in the Light of Neorealism*. Princeton: Princeton University Press, 1986.

Masi, Stefano, and Enrico Lancia. *I film di Roberto Rossellini*. Rome: Gremese Editore, 1987.

Miccichè, Lino, ed. *Cinema italiano degli anni '70: cronache 1969–78*. Venice: Marsilio Editori, 1980.

Il cinema italiano degli anni '60. Venice: Marsilio Editori, 1975.

Il neorealismo cinematografico italiano. Venice: Marsilio Editori, 1975.

Monaco, James. *How to Read a Film: The Art, Technology, Language, History, and Theory of Film and Media*. New York: Oxford University Press, 1977.

Overbey, David, ed. *Springtime in Italy: A Reader on Neorealism*. Hamden, Conn.: Archon Books, 1979.

Quaglietti, Lorenzo. *Storia economico-politica del cinema italiano, 1945–1980*. Rome: Editori Riuniti, 1980.

Ranvaud, Dan, ed. *Roberto Rossellini*. British Film Institute Dossier no. 8. London, 1981.

Redi, Riccardo, ed. *Cinema italiano sotto il fascismo*. Venice: Marsilio Editori, 1979.

Redi, Riccardo, and Claudio Camerini, eds. *Cinecittà 1: industria e mercato nel cinema italiano tra le due guerre*. Venice: Marsilio Editori, 1985.

Roberto Rossellini. Rome: Ente Autonomo di Gestione per il Cinema, 1987 [catalogue for retrospective at Houston, Texas].

Rohdie, Sam. "Capital and Realism in the Italian Cinema: An Examination of Film in the Fascist Period." *Screen* 24, no. 4–5 (1983), 37–46.

Rondolino, Gianni. "Italian Propaganda Films: 1940–1943." In K. R. M. Short, ed., *Film and Radio Propaganda in World War II*, pp. 230–44. Knoxville: University of Tennessee Press, 1983.

Roberto Rossellini. Florence: La Nuova Italia, 1974.

Roberto Rossellini. Turin: UTET, 1989.

Rossellini, Roberto. *Le cinéma révélé*. Edited by Alain Bergala. Paris: Editions de l'Etoile, 1984 [French versions of French interviews with Rossellini].

"A Discussion of Neo-Realism: Rossellini Interviewed by Mario Verdone." *Screen* 14, no. 4 (1973–74), 69–77.

Era notte a Roma. Edited by Renzo Renzi. Bologna: Cappelli, 1960.

Un esprit libre ne doit rien apprendre en esclave. Paris: Fayard, 1977.

"An Interview with Roberto Rossellini by Adriano Aprà and Maurizio Ponzi." *Screen* 14, no. 4 (1973–74), 112–26.

Il mio metodo. Edited by Adriano Aprà. Venice: Marsilio Editori, 1987 [Italian edition of Rossellini's major interviews and writings on the cinema].

"A Panorama of History: Interview with Rossellini by Francisco Llinas and Miguel Marias with Antonio Drove and Jos Oliver." *Screen* 14, no. 4 (1973–74), 83–109.

Quasi un'autobiografia. Edited by Stefano Roncoroni. Milan: Mondadori, 1987. French edition: *Fragments d'une autobiographie.* Paris: Editions Ramsay, 1987.

"Rossellini on Rossellini." *Screen* 14, no. 4 (1973–74), 79–81.

"Rossellini's Manifesto." *Screen* 14, no. 4 (1973–74), 110–11.

La trilogia della guerra. Edited by Stefano Roncoroni. Bologna: Cappelli, 1972.

Utopia autopsia 10'°. Rome: Armando Editore, 1974.

The War Trilogy. Edited by Stefano Roncoroni. New York: Grossman, 1973.

Rossi, Patrizio. *Roberto Rossellini: A Guide to References and Resources.* Boston: G. K. Hall, 1988 [bibliography of Rossellini materials to 1978].

Sanders, George. *Memoirs of a Professional Cad.* New York: Putnam's, 1960.

Sarris, Andrew. "Rossellini Rediscovered." *Film Culture* 32 (1964), 60–63.

Savio, Francesco. *Cinecittà anni trenta: parlano 116 protagonisti del secondo cinema italiano (1930–1943).* 3 vols. Rome: Bulzoni, 1979.

Ma l'amore no: realismo, formalismo, propaganda e telefoni bianchi nel cinema italiano di regime (1930–1943). Milan: Sonzogno, 1975.

Serceau, Michel. *Roberto Rossellini.* Paris: Editions du Cerf, 1986.

Short, K. R. M., ed. *Film and Radio Propaganda in World War II.* Knoxville: University of Tennessee Press, 1983.

Sinclair, Michael. "Ellipsis in Rossellini's *Paisà:* The Privileging of the Invisible." *Spectator* 9, no. 1 (1988), 38–55.

Sorlin, Pierre. *European Cinemas, European Societies, 1939–1990.* New York: Routledge, 1991.

The Film in History: Restaging the Past. Oxford: Basil Blackwell, 1980 [Italian films on the Risorgimento and the Resistance].

Trasatti, Sergio. *Rossellini e la televisione.* Rome: La Rassegna Editrice, 1978.

Verdone, Mario. *Roberto Rossellini.* Paris: Editions Séghers, 1963.

Vivere il cinema: cinquant'anni del Centro sperimentale di cinematografia. Rome: Presidenza del Consiglio dei Ministri, 1987.

Walsh, Martin. "Re-evaluating Rossellini." *Jump Cut* 15 (1977) 13–15. Reprinted in Dan Ranvaud, ed., *Roberto Rossellini,* pp. 51–55. British Film Institute Dossier no. 8. London, 1981.

Index

The following index lists under the director's name all films discussed in the book and does not contain references to material in the notes.

De Filippo, Eduardo, 93
De Gasperi, Alcide, 26, 29
De Marchis, Marcella, 2
DeMenil, Dominique and Jean, 28
De Robertis, Francesco, 11, 12, 34, 36, 47,
   83; *Alfa Tau!* 11; *Uomini sul fondo*,
   11
De Santis, Giuseppe, 7, 12, 40–41
Descartes, René, 26
De Sica, Vittorio, 2, 8, 13, 24, 49, 62, 83,
   86, 119–24; *I bambini ci guardano*,
   83; *Ladri di biciclette*, 49, 86, 119;
   Miracolo a Milano, 86; *Sciuscià*, 119
Di Donato, Pietro, 15
Di Giammatteo, Fernaldo, 87, 129
Direzione generale per la cinematografia, 5,
   11
Dmytryk, Edward, 15

Edmonds, Dale, 68
Eisenstein, Sergei, 38, 99, 107
Erlanger, Philippe, 128

Fabbri, Diego, 112
Fabrizi, Aldo, 49, 52, 119
Feist, Harry, 49
Fellini, Federico, 12, 15, 16, 20, 28, 30–31,
   45, 47–48, 49, 52–53, 65, 66, 68, 76,
   77, 80, 83, 85, 111, 117; *Amarcord*,
   117; *I clowns*, 28; *Le notti di Cabiria*,
   16; *La strada*, 16
Freddi, Luigi, 5, 10–11, 34
French New Wave, 30, 31, 99, 115

Gassman, Vittorio, 115
Geiger, Rod, 48, 68, 76
Genina, Augusto, 8, 9–11, 83; *L'assedio
   dell'Alcazar*, 9–11, 83; *Lo squadrone
   bianco*, 8
Gioventù universitaria fascista, 6
Girotti, Massimo, 34, 36
Giuliani, Reginaldo, 36
Godard, Jean-Luc, 22, 62, 63, 99, 100, 127,
   128, 136; *Le mépris*, 100
Grant, Cary, 121
Gravelli, Asvero, 32
Gregoretti, Ugo, 23
Griffith, D. W., 62, 99
Guarner, José, 101

Hayes, Alfred, 76
Hitchcock, Alfred, 123
Honegger, Arthur, 22
Hughes, Howard, 18

Istituto Luce (L'unione cinematografica
   educativa), 5, 11
Italian Communist Party, 29

Jappolo, Beniamino, 22
Johnson, Dots, 68

Lang, Fritz, 129
Lenin, Vladimir, 5, 6
Leone, Sergio, 130
Lisandrini, Antonio, 17
Lizzani, Carlo, 3, 7
Longanesi, Leo, 7
Louis XIV, 26, 27–30, 124, 130–37

Machiavelli, Niccolò, 136
Magnani, Anna, 13, 14, 15, 18, 49, 87
Manet, Claude, 99, 101
Mankiewicz, Joseph, 130
Mann, Anthony, 130
Mann, Klaus, 13
Marc'Aurelio, 52
Marx, Karl, 26, 29
Masina, Giulietta, 66
Mastroianni, Marcello, 116
Matisse, Henri, 100, 101
Mattoli, Mario, 11
Michi, Maria, 49
Mida, Massimo, 68
Miller, Arthur, 22
Ministero per la cultura popolare, 5
Monicelli, Mario, 112, 116; *I compagni*,
   116; *La grande guerra*, 112
Montanelli, Indro, 112
Moore, Gar, 68
Moravia, Alberto, 100
Morlion, Félix, 17
Moro, Aldo, 29
Morosini, Giuseppe, 52
Mursino, Tito Silvio: *see* Mussolini, Vittorio
Mussolini, Benito, 4, 5, 32, 35, 38, 78, 116
Mussolini, Bruno, 11
Mussolini, Vittorio, 3, 6, 7, 11, 32, 42

NASA, 28
NATO, 29
NBC, 27
Negroni, Baldassare, 119–20
Noris, Assia, 2

Olmi, Ermanno, 31
ORTF, 27
Oscars, 16

Pagliero, Marcello, 1, 49
Pagnol, Marcel, 16
Pascal, Blaise, 26
Pasolini, Pier Paolo, 23, 31, 49, 115
Passarelli, Edoardo, 49
Patte, Jean-Marie, 134
Pavolini, Alessandro, 11